Broadcast Schedule

Solomon

January 31–February 21, 1995

Tuesday	January 31	Stepping into Big Sandals Selected Scriptures
Wednesday	February 1	Stepping into Big Sandals
Thursday	February 2	Solomon in Living Color Selected Scriptures from 1 Kings
Friday	February 3	Solomon in Living Color

Monday	February 6	Signs of Erosion Selected Scriptures
Tuesday	February 7	Signs of Erosion
Wednesday	February 8	When the Heart Is Turned Away 1 Kings 11:1–9
Thursday	February 9	When the Heart Is Turned Away
Friday	February 10	How God Deals with Defiance 1 Kings 11:9–28, 40

Monday	February 13	How God Deals with Defiance
Tuesday	February 14	Sound Advice from an Old Rebel Ecclesiastes 11:9–12:7
Wednesday	February 15	Sound Advice from an Old Rebel
Thursday	February 16	A Plea for Godliness Selected Scriptures
Friday	February 17	A Plea for Godliness

| Monday | February 20 | Needed: A Godly Mind
Ephesians 6:10–13; 2 Corinthians 2:10–11;
4:3–4; 10:3–5 |
| Tuesday | February 21 | Needed: A Godly Mind |

Insight for Living • Post Office Box 69000, Anaheim, CA 92817-0900
Insight for Living Ministries • Post Office Box 2510, Vancouver, BC, Canada V6B 3W7
Insight for Living, Inc. • GPO Box 2823 EE, Melbourne, VIC 3001, Australia

Printed in the United States of America

Solomon

BIBLE STUDY GUIDE

From the Bible-teaching ministry of

Charles R. Swindoll

INSIGHT FOR LIVING

Chuck graduated in 1963 from Dallas Theological Seminary, where he now serves as the school's fourth president, helping to prepare a new generation of men and women for the ministry. Chuck has served in pastorates in three states: Massachusetts, Texas, and California, including almost twenty-three years at the First Evangelical Free Church in Fullerton, California. His sermon messages have been aired over radio since 1979 as the *Insight for Living* broadcast. A best-selling author, Chuck has written numerous books and booklets on many subjects.

Based on the outlines and transcripts of Chuck's sermons, the study guide text is co-authored by Ken Gire, a graduate of Texas Christian University and Dallas Theological Seminary.

Editor in Chief:
Cynthia Swindoll

Coauthor of Text:
Ken Gire

Assistant Editor:
Wendy Peterson

Copy Editor:
Tom Kimber

Text Designer:
Gary Lett

Publishing System Specialist:
Alex Pasieka

Director, Communications and Marketing Division:
Deedee Snyder

Marketing Manager:
Alene Cooper

Project Coordinator:
Colette Muse

Production Manager:
John Norton

Printer:
Sinclair Printing Company

Unless otherwise identified, all Scripture references are from the New American Standard Bible, © The Lockman Foundation 1960, 1962, 1963, 1968, 1971, 1972, 1973, 1975, 1977. Used by permission. Scripture taken from the Holy Bible, New International Version, © 1973, 1978, 1984 International Bible Society, used by permission of Zondervan Bible Publishers. The other translations cited are The Living Bible [LB] and Amplified Bible [AMPLIFIED].

An effort has been made to locate sources and obtain permission where necessary for the quotations used in this book. In the event of any unintentional omission, a modification will gladly be incorporated in future printings.

ISBN 0-8499-8588-9
COVER DESIGN: Nina Paris
COVER PAINTING: *Solomon and the Queen of Sheba* by Erasmus Quellin II, Giraudon/Art Resource, N.Y.
Printed in the United States of America

CONTENTS

*These messages were not a part of the original series but are compatible with it.

INTRODUCTION

Erosion is not limited to soil along the banks of a river. It can happen in life as well. Slow and silent like a stream, it sweeps away character a grain of sand at a time. From a distance, the landscape appears so tranquil and serene, but a closer look reveals the surging washout of integrity and morality.

So it was with Solomon. Born with all the benefits, blessed with a bright, creative mind and keen abilities, the man who suddenly became a king slowly became a fool. Call it whatever you wish—sowing wild oats, mid-life crisis, spiritual defection, or just plain carnality—Solomon's passions broke their banks in a flood of immorality and idolatry. And for the rest of his life, he was busy mopping up the consequences.

From his gold crown to his clay feet, Solomon is thoroughly examined in our first six lessons. Not only do they depict his rich-and-famous lifestyle, but his subsequent moral bankruptcy as well. Listen closely. Think deeply. And lest we think we stand tall and upright by comparison, there are also two penetrating New Testament studies to keep us on our knees.

Chuck Swindoll

Chuck Swindoll

PUTTING TRUTH INTO ACTION

K nowledge apart from application falls short of God's desire for His children. He wants us to apply what we learn so that we will change and grow. This study guide was prepared with these goals in mind. As you go through the following pages, we hope your desire to discover biblical truth will grow as your understanding of God's Word increases and that you will be encouraged to apply what you've learned.

To assist you in your study, we've included a section called 👑 **Living Insights** at the end of each lesson. These exercises will challenge you to study further and to think of specific ways to put your discoveries into action.

There are many ways to use this guide—in personal devotions, group studies, discussions with friends and family, and Sunday school classes. And, of course, it's an ideal study aid when you're listening to its corresponding *Insight for Living* radio series.

To benefit most from this study guide, we would encourage you to consider it a spiritual journal. That's why we've included space in the **Living Insights** for recording your thoughts and discoveries. We hope you'll return to those sections often for review and encouragement as you continue to grow in your walk with Christ.

Ken Gire

Ken Gire
Coauthor

Solomon

Chapter 1

STEPPING INTO BIG SANDALS

Selected Scriptures

Compared to Solomon's splendor, *Lifestyles of the Rich and Famous* looks like life on skid row! Those "champagne wishes" and "caviar dreams" wilt like faded flowers next to the dazzling display of his prosperity and power.

Under Solomon, Jerusalem glistened like a brilliant gem between the liquid sapphire of the Mediterranean and the mineral-rich sparkle of the Dead Sea. This scintillating jewel was the central stone of the empire, where peace radiantly shone for forty years. Indeed, during Solomon's reign, Jerusalem was "a city set on a hill"—a light to the world.

But Solomon's renown went beyond his wealth and extended to his wisdom as well. His fame spilled over the borders of Israel to inundate the entire Middle East. So incredible were the reports that the queen of Sheba herself journeyed from her kingdom in Africa to verify the source of this flood of rumors. Her breath was literally taken away when she saw Solomon's wisdom and glory.

> And when the queen of Sheba had seen the wisdom of Solomon, the house which he had built, the food at his table, the seating of his servants, the attendance of his ministers and their attire, his cupbearers and their attire, and his stairway by which he went up to the house of the Lord, she was breathless. Then she said to the king, "It was a true report which I heard in my own land about your words and your wisdom. Nevertheless I did not believe their reports until I came and my eyes had seen it. And behold, the

half of the greatness of your wisdom was not told me. You surpass the report that I heard." (2 Chron. 9:3–6)

News of Solomon's greatness still circulated in Israel during the time of Christ. In Matthew, Jesus speaks both of Solomon's glory (6:29) and of the greatness of his wisdom (12:42). Even today, Solomon's glory still gilds our perception. Granted, there is much to eschew about his life—his eroding character, his errant ways. But there is also much to emulate.

"Long Live King Solomon!"

The turmoil of his father David's home nearly snatched the throne from Solomon. One brother, Adonijah, connived with several of their father's advisers and was making preparations to have himself declared king. But those loyal to David stuck by Solomon and informed the king of Adonijah's scheme (1 Kings 1:1–27). David, who had already chosen Solomon as his successor, immediately took steps to safeguard this son's future.

> Then King David answered and said, "Call Bathsheba to me." And she came into the king's presence and stood before the king. And the king vowed and said, "As the Lord lives, who has redeemed my life from all distress, surely as I vowed to you by the Lord the God of Israel, saying, 'Your son Solomon shall be king after me, and he shall sit on my throne in my place'; I will indeed do so this day." . . . Then King David said, "Call to me Zadok the priest, Nathan the prophet, and Benaiah the son of Jehoiada." And they came into the king's presence. And the king said to them, "Take with you the servants of your lord, and have my son Solomon ride on my own mule, and bring him down to Gihon. And let Zadok the priest and Nathan the prophet anoint him there as king over Israel, and blow the trumpet and say, 'Long live King Solomon!'" (1 Kings 1:28–30, 32–34)

With that clarion call, a golden age of peace and prosperity stepped through the gates of Jerusalem—an age that rested upon the shoulders of a young king who had been groomed for the throne since his boyhood.

His Birth and Name

After the storm of David's adultery with Bathsheba; in the wake of deception, murder, and cover-up (2 Sam. 11–12); and after a period of withering health and misery (Ps. 32), a calm came in the form of a son.

> Then David comforted his wife Bathsheba, and went in to her and lay with her; and she gave birth to a son, and he named him Solomon.[1] Now the Lord loved him and sent word through Nathan the prophet, and he named him Jedidiah[2] for the Lord's sake. (2 Sam. 12:24–25)

His Childhood and Training

Since God used Nathan to confer a special name upon Solomon, it is possible that the prophet was the young boy's tutor. Doubtless, however, Solomon's impressionable ears picked up other messages that loitered around his home—messages noting wickedness, tension, pride, and deception: Amnon's rape of his half sister Tamar, Absalom's rebellion, David's sin of numbering the people. And, as rumors die hard, hushed whispers of his father's checkered past probably still echoed through the marbled halls of the king's palace where Solomon grew up.

His Inauguration and Reign

Commentator Alfred Edersheim estimates that Solomon was probably twenty-five at most when he became king.[3] Yet, Solomon was still able to make prosperity, loyalty, and majesty the hallmarks of his reign.

> Then Solomon sat on the throne of the Lord as king instead of David his father; and he prospered, and all Israel obeyed him. And all the officials, the mighty men, and also all the sons of King David pledged allegiance to King Solomon. And the Lord

---

1. The Hebrew word for Solomon—*Shelomoh*—comes from the root *shalem*, which is a derivative of *shalom*, meaning "peace."

2. The name Jedidiah means "loved by Jehovah."

3. Alfred Edersheim, *The Bible History: Old Testament* (Grand Rapids, Mich.: William B. Eerdmans Publishing Co., 1959), vol. 5, pp. 56–57.

highly exalted Solomon in the sight of all Israel, and bestowed on him royal majesty which had not been on any king before him in Israel. (1 Chron. 29:23–25)

For forty years, from about 970–930 B.C., Solomon sat on the throne of a united Israel, where all the people "lived in safety, every man under his vine and his fig tree, from Dan even to Beersheba, all the days of Solomon" (1 Kings 4:25).

"The Lord His God Was with Him"

Over in 2 Chronicles, we see the reason Solomon became so great: "The Lord his God was with him and exalted him greatly" (1:1b). During Solomon's reign, God showered him with the blessings of wisdom and knowledge, discernment and strength, riches and fame, vision and skill.

Giving Him Wisdom and Knowledge

At a time when Solomon's heart was tender toward God, a solitary pact between the two took place.

In that night God appeared to Solomon and said to him, "Ask what I shall give you." And Solomon said to God, "Thou hast dealt with my father David with great lovingkindness, and hast made me king in his place. Now, O Lord God, Thy promise to my father David is fulfilled; for Thou hast made me king over a people as numerous as the dust of the earth. Give me now wisdom and knowledge, that I may go out and come in before this people; for who can rule this great people of Thine?" And God said to Solomon, "Because you had this in mind, and did not ask for riches, wealth, or honor, or the life of those who hate you, nor have you even asked for long life, but you have asked for yourself wisdom and knowledge, that you may rule My people, over whom I have made you king, wisdom and knowledge have been granted to you. And I will give you riches and wealth and honor, such as none of the kings who were before you has possessed, nor those who will come after you." (2 Chron. 1:7–12)

4

Giving Him Discernment and Strength

In addition to having these administrative gifts, Solomon was a poet, songwriter, and a lover of nature.

> Now God gave Solomon wisdom and very great discernment and breadth of mind, like the sand that is on the seashore. And Solomon's wisdom surpassed the wisdom of all the sons of the east and all the wisdom of Egypt. For he was wiser than all men, . . . and his fame was known in all the surrounding nations. He also spoke 3,000 proverbs, and his songs were 1,005. And he spoke of trees, from the cedar that is in Lebanon even to the hyssop that grows on the wall; he spoke also of animals and birds and creeping things and fish. And men came from all peoples to hear the wisdom of Solomon, from all the kings of the earth who had heard of his wisdom.[4]
> (1 Kings 4:29–34)

Giving Him Riches and Fame

Solomon's wealth was made up of a diversified portfolio of income, assets, and gifts.

> Judah and Israel were as numerous as the sand that is on the seashore in abundance; they were eating and drinking and rejoicing.
> Now Solomon ruled over all the kingdoms from the River to the land of the Philistines and to the border of Egypt; they brought tribute and served Solomon all the days of his life. And Solomon's provision for one day was thirty kors[5] of fine flour and sixty kors of meal, ten fat oxen, twenty pasture-fed oxen, a hundred sheep besides deer, gazelles, roebucks, and fattened fowl. For he had dominion over everything west of the River, from Tiphsah even

---

4. A classic example of his wisdom is found in the familiar passage of 1 Kings 3:16–28, where he settles a dispute between two women claiming to be the mother of the same child.

5. A kor was equivalent to six bushels. See "Table of Weights and Measures" in the *NIV Study Bible*, gen. ed. Kenneth Barker (Grand Rapids, Mich.: Zondervan Bible Publishers, 1985), n.p.

to Gaza, over all the kings west of the River; and he had peace on all sides around about him. So Judah and Israel lived in safety, every man under his vine and his fig tree, from Dan even to Beersheba, all the days of Solomon. And Solomon had 40,000 stalls of horses for his chariots, and 12,000 horsemen. And those deputies provided for King Solomon and all who came to King Solomon's table, each in his month; they left nothing lacking. (1 Kings 4:20–27)

"The king made silver as common as stones in Jerusalem" (10:27), so for his palace he used only the finest gold.

Now the weight of gold which came in to Solomon in one year was 666 talents[6] of gold, besides that from the traders and the wares of the merchants and all the kings of the Arabs and the governors of the country. And King Solomon made 200 large shields of beaten gold, using 600 shekels of gold on each large shield. And he made 300 shields of beaten gold, using three minas of gold on each shield, and the king put them in the house of the forest of Lebanon. Moreover, the king made a great throne of ivory and overlaid it with refined gold. There were six steps to the throne and a round top to the throne at its rear, and arms on each side of the seat, and two lions standing beside the arms. And twelve lions were standing there on the six steps on the one side and on the other; nothing like it was made for any other kingdom. And all King Solomon's drinking vessels were of gold, and all the vessels of the house of the forest of Lebanon were of pure gold. None was of silver; it was not considered valuable in the days of Solomon. For the king had at sea the ships of Tarshish with the ships of Hiram; once every three years the ships of Tarshish came bringing gold and silver, ivory and apes and peacocks. (1 Kings 10: 14–22)

---

6. These 666 talents amounted to nearly 25 tons. See the NIV Study Bible, p. 492, note n.

Giving Him Vision and Skill

Solomon's reputation stretched across continents and brought back hungry audiences eager to catch the morsels of wisdom that fell from his lips.

> So King Solomon became greater than all the kings of the earth in riches and in wisdom. And all the earth was seeking the presence of Solomon, to hear his wisdom which God had put in his heart. (1 Kings 10:23–24)

"Forget None of His Benefits"

Solomon, obviously, was uniquely gifted. And it's human nature, when abundantly blessed, to forget the source of our benefits. An echo from Solomon's father, David, exhorts us in Psalm 103:

> Bless the Lord, O my soul;
> And all that is within me, bless His holy name.
> Bless the Lord, O my soul,
> And forget none of His benefits. (vv. 1–2)

What are some of His benefits? Drawing from Solomon's example, there are at least four.

First, *our minds*. We may not have Solomon's singular treasure trove of wisdom, but we have the same Lord who dispenses wisdom "to all men generously and without reproach" if we only ask (James 1:5). God has gifted us with the capacity to think, to learn, to understand, to become wise. We need to take the time both to cultivate the gift of our mind and to thank God for it.

Second, *our stability*. We are more used to being reproved for not standing firm, aren't we? Let's turn that around right now and recall those experiences when we *have* used discernment and strength to hang in there through tough times. We need to remember those stretching, growing periods when we persevered and let God build character in us. And we need to thank Him for enabling us to remain stable in the midst of uncertainty and pain.

Third, *our possessions*. Have we become more guilty than grateful for the nice things God has graciously provided us? For a good job? For increased sales? For a wonderful promotion? God didn't shame Solomon for his riches—God gave Solomon those riches! Of course, we're to set our hearts not on what has been provided but on Who has provided, and we're to enjoy His gifts with gratitude.

And fourth, *our hope*. Because of Jesus, we have an eternal vision, a perspective that not only gives us hope of heaven but also hope in our daily, temporal lives. We can learn to see good from bad, better from best, and we've been equipped with spiritual skills to bring our God-given dreams into reality. Often our dreams involve the lives and futures of our children, so we must take the time to build into them those qualities that will last in God's kingdom. And we must thank the Lord for giving us high ideals and hopes to reach for.

It's so easy to rush ahead to the failures of Solomon's later life. But let's not skip over the God-recorded fact that he was highly blessed. And so are we.

> Bless the Lord, all you His hosts,
> You who serve Him, doing His will.
> Bless the Lord, all you works of His,
> In all places of His dominion;
> Bless the Lord, O my soul! (Ps. 103:21–22)

👑 *Living Insights* STUDY ONE

Proverbs, written largely by Solomon, is a prism through which wisdom shines and refracts a rainbow of multi-hued meanings. One of these shadings is found in chapter 8, where wisdom is personified as a woman calling to passersby in the street. We are told that she

- "is better than jewels; And all desirable things can not compare with her" (v. 11);

- that prudence, knowledge, and discretion are her roommates (v. 12);

- that by her "kings reign, And rulers decree justice" (v. 15);

- that "riches and honor" accompany her (v. 18);

- and that he who finds her "obtains favor from the Lord" (v. 35).

God may not have entrusted you with a great kingdom to rule as He did Solomon, but He has entrusted some of His people to you—your family. Do you recognize them before God, as Solomon did Israel, as "this great people of Thine" rather than yours to

8

control and own (see 2 Chron. 1:10)? What is your attitude toward your family?

_____

_____

_____

Are you guiding and serving them with godly wisdom, or do your own ideas of who they should be and what they should do dominate your relationship with them? Give a recent example of an exchange between you and one of your children.

_____

_____

_____

If you find that your parenting perspective is a bit more limited than you'd like it to be, take a cue from Solomon and ask God for His wisdom. Ask Him to help you train your eye to His perspective. Ask Him to help you see your family as His people, with a purpose He has designed specifically for each of them. And ask Him to help you discern earthly wisdom from true wisdom.

> Who among you is wise and understanding? Let him show by his good behavior his deeds in the gentleness of wisdom. But if you have bitter jealousy and selfish ambition in your heart, do not be arrogant and so lie against the truth. This wisdom is not that which comes down from above, but is earthly, natural, demonic. For where jealousy and selfish ambition exist, there is disorder and every evil thing. But the wisdom from above is first pure, then peaceable, gentle, reasonable, full of mercy and good fruits, unwavering, without hypocrisy. And the seed whose fruit is righteousness is sown in peace by those who make peace. (James 3:13–18)

David's lyrics of gratitude in Psalm 103 inspire us to bless the Lord with all that is within us too! Right now, take time to count your blessings. You may want to begin with the list at the end of our lesson—your mind, your stability, your possessions, your hope— then branch out from there and go wherever your heart leads you. Write down all your benefits, however small they may be, and then return to this personal psalm for encouragement and remembrance.

_____

_____

_____

_____

_____

_____

_____

_____

_____

_____

_____

Chapter 2

SOLOMON IN
LIVING COLOR

Selected Scriptures from 1 Kings

Typecasting. No matter how versatile or talented some actors are, their entire careers can be straitjacketed if they're typecast into certain roles. Edward G. Robinson, for example, was rarely seen outside his roles as a ruthless gangster. Similarly, the name Boris Karloff became synonymous with sinister parts in scary movies. And after *Dracula*, one wonders if Bela Lugosi was ever considered for the lead of a serious, romantic drama—he was forever typecast into vampirish roles.

Sometimes we do that with people in real life too. Thomas was a faithful disciple of Jesus for three long, hard years. Yet, because of one moment of skepticism after the Resurrection, we have typecast him as Doubting Thomas. Solomon has also been unfairly dealt with by biblical historians. Most focus on his later, declining years as if his entire life were one massive shipwreck. However, as we read the opening chapters of his biography, we find the opposite— a young, eager king with a tender heart for the things of the Lord.

Solomon—Man of God

The early stages of Solomon's reign highlight with explicit clarity that God was with him.

> Now Solomon the son of David established himself securely over his kingdom, and the Lord his God was with him and exalted him greatly. (2 Chron. 1:1)

Solomon actively cultivated his relationship with God. The genuineness of his heart is especially revealed in his private response to the Father, which was characterized by childlike dependence.

> "And now, O Lord my God, Thou hast made Thy servant king in place of my father David, yet I am but a little child; I do not know how to go out or come in. And Thy servant is in the midst of Thy people which Thou hast chosen, a great people who

cannot be numbered or counted for multitude. So give Thy servant an understanding heart to judge Thy people to discern between good and evil. For who is able to judge this great people of Thine?" (1 Kings 3:7–9)

As a natural outgrowth of his private relationship with God, Solomon's public confession of faith was unashamedly open.

> And it came about that when Solomon had finished praying this entire prayer and supplication to the Lord, he arose from before the altar of the Lord, from kneeling on his knees with his hands spread toward heaven. And he stood and blessed all the assembly of Israel with a loud voice, saying, "Blessed be the Lord, who has given rest to His people Israel, according to all that He promised; not one word has failed of all His good promise, which He promised through Moses His servant. May the Lord our God be with us, as He was with our fathers; may He not leave us or forsake us, that He may incline our hearts to Himself, to walk in all His ways and to keep His commandments and His statutes and His ordinances, which He commanded our fathers. And may these words of mine, with which I have made supplication before the Lord, be near to the Lord our God day and night, that He may maintain the cause of His servant and the cause of His people Israel, as each day requires, so that all the peoples of the earth may know that the Lord is God; there is no one else. Let your heart therefore be wholly devoted to the Lord our God, to walk in His statutes and to keep His commandments, as at this day." (1 Kings 8:54–61)

Genuine humility. Personal integrity. Scriptural loyalty. If we were to typecast Solomon, these are the qualities we would want to focus on.

Solomon—Author and Composer

Solomon was a Renaissance man in every sense of the word— his interests were broad; his intelligence, deep.

Now God gave Solomon wisdom and very great discernment and breadth of mind, like the sand that is on the seashore. And Solomon's wisdom surpassed the wisdom of all the sons of the east and all the wisdom of Egypt. For he was wiser than all men, than Ethan the Ezrahite, Heman, Calcol and Darda, the sons of Mahol; and his fame was known in all the surrounding nations. He also spoke 3,000 proverbs, and his songs were 1,005. And he spoke of trees, from the cedar that is in Lebanon even to the hyssop that grows on the wall; he spoke also of animals and birds and creeping things and fish. And men came from all peoples to hear the wisdom of Solomon, from all the kings of the earth who had heard of his wisdom. (1 Kings 4:29–34)

Just look at his interests: writing, composition, botany, and various branches of zoology. Commentator C. F. Keil gives us even further insight into Solomon's range of expertise. Where "the sons of the east" were "celebrated for their astronomy and astrology," the proverbial "wisdom of the Egyptians" encompassed

the most diverse branches of knowledge, such as geometry, arithmetic, astronomy, and astrology . . . , and as their skill in the preparation of ointments from vegetable and animal sources, and their extensive acquaintance with medicine, clearly prove, embraced natural science as well, in which Solomon, according to verse 33, was very learned.[1]

Solomon's peers included Ethan the Ezrahite, Heman, and Calcol and Darda, who were the sons of Mahol. Faceless names to us today, but these were the Einsteins . . . the Nobel and Pulitzer Prize winners . . . the intellectual elite of that day. In Solomon, then, we find authentic spirituality wedded to academic excellence. These qualities give birth to an appreciation for beauty, diversity, and creativity.

---

1. C. F. Keil, *The Books of the Kings*, trans. James Martin, in *Biblical Commentary on the Old Testament*, by C. F. Keil and F. Delitzsch (Grand Rapids, Mich.: William B. Eerdmans Publishing Co., n.d.), p. 55.

Solomon—Administrator and Architect

Not only was Solomon a man of God, an artist, and a scholar—
he was a skilled administrator as well. Chapter 4 of 1 Kings reveals
his herculean task: "Now King Solomon was king over all Israel"
(v. 1). As a wise administrator, he divided his many responsibilities into manageable pieces, delegating the tasks to capable men.
Verses 2–6 list Solomon's officials, while verses 7–19 list his twelve
deputies.[2]

Solomon's administrative gifts were also utilized in the architectural realm. His projects included houses, reservoirs, gardens,
parks, orchards, and vineyards (Eccles. 2:4–6). However, the most
noted jewel in his architectural crown was the temple he built for
the Lord (1 Kings 6).[3] The project was not massive, at least in size.
The temple was only ninety feet long, thirty feet wide, and forty-
five feet high (v. 2).[4] But in scope, the task took a marathon seven
and a half years to complete (vv. 37–38).

Though unimpressive in size, the craftsmanship was exceedingly
elaborate. A porch led into the main sanctuary (v. 3), and "for the
house he made windows with artistic frames" (v. 4). For Solomon,
form was as important as function; beauty, as important as utility.
The doors were not made simply to open and close; they were
adorned with intricate carvings of cherubim, gourds, palm trees,
and open flowers to please the eye and lift the spirit (vv. 18, 32).
The attention paid to artistic detail was painstaking, as was the
method of construction.

> And the house, while it was being built, was built
> of stone prepared at the quarry, and there was nei-
> ther hammer nor axe nor any iron tool heard in the
> house while it was being built. (v. 7)

An unhurried but serious reverence paced the workers and per-
meated the atmosphere on the construction site. Gold was used to
cover the entire temple symbolizing the value of worship and
fellowship with God.

2. Other examples of Solomon's administrative abilities can be found in 1 Kings 5:13–18
and 9:15–23.

3. For a detailed description, consult *The Zondervan Pictorial Encyclopedia of the Bible*, gen.
ed. Merrill C. Tenney (Grand Rapids, Mich.: Zondervan Publishing House, 1976), vol. 5, p.
472.

4. The Bible lists the temple's dimensions in cubits—a cubit being equivalent to eighteen inches.

So Solomon overlaid the inside of the house with pure gold. And he drew chains of gold across the front of the inner sanctuary; and he overlaid it with gold. And he overlaid the whole house with gold, until all the house was finished. Also the whole altar which was by the inner sanctuary he overlaid with gold. (vv. 21–22)

Solomon—Diplomat and Businessman

We have seen Solomon as an authentic man of God, author, academician, administrator, and architect. Now we will observe him in arenas ranging from making allies to trading horses.

Making Allies

Like all leaders, Solomon occasionally needed to do the delicate work of creating and maintaining alliances. One such alliance was with Hiram.

> Now Hiram king of Tyre sent his servants to Solomon, when he heard that they had anointed him king in place of his father, for Hiram had always been a friend of David. (1 Kings 5:1)

When Solomon came to the throne, his relationship with Hiram was uncertain, because Hiram didn't know whether the new king would maintain his father's alliances. Solomon, however, wisely worked out a business transaction that would put the relationship on solid footing.

> So Hiram gave Solomon as much as he desired of the cedar and cypress timber. Solomon then gave Hiram 20,000 kors of wheat as food for his household, and twenty kors of beaten oil; thus Solomon would give Hiram year by year. And the Lord gave wisdom to Solomon, just as He promised him; and there was peace between Hiram and Solomon, and the two of them made a covenant. (vv. 10–12)

Making Trades

Solomon's interests in horses extended as far as Egypt in procuring the best for his chariots and horsemen.

Now Solomon gathered chariots and horsemen; and he had 1,400 chariots and 12,000 horsemen, and he stationed them in the chariot cities and with the king in Jerusalem. . . . Also Solomon's import of horses was from Egypt and Kue, and the king's merchants procured them from Kue for a price. And a chariot was imported from Egypt for 600 shekels of silver, and a horse for 150; and by the same means they exported them to all the kings of the Hittites and to the kings of the Arameans. (1 Kings 10:26, 28–29)

Again, in choosing the best animals and in making the best deals, insightful wisdom was paramount.

Emulating Solomon

As we wrap up this thumbnail sketch of Solomon, we see that he was indeed a multitalented, live-life-to-the-hilt type of person. He used the gifts God had given him to the fullest . . . and by doing so, gave glory to God. The exhortation of this lesson is to emulate Solomon. Franky Schaeffer gives us a word of challenge along these lines.

By exercising those talents God has given you, you are praising him. Whether what you express is "religious" or "secular," as a Christian you are praising him. Everything is his. . . .

Remember that as a creative person, the important thing is to create. Who sees what you make, where it goes and what it does is a secondary consideration; the first is to exercise the talent God has given you.[5]

Living Insights

Solomon's temple was an architectural triumph of beauty and utility. Since it was the sanctuary of God—the place where God

5. Franky Schaeffer, *Addicted to Mediocrity: 20th Century Christians and the Arts* (Westchester, Ill.: Crossway Books, 1981), pp. 59–60.

dwelt—only the best materials and artisans were accepted for the project. Technically, God does not dwell among people today in the same way He did during Old Testament times. Instead, under the new covenant, "*we* are the temple of the living God" (2 Cor. 6:16, emphasis added). In his first letter to the Corinthians, Paul details what this means.

> According to the grace of God which was given to me, as a wise master builder I laid a foundation, and another is building upon it. But let each man be careful how he builds upon it. For no man can lay a foundation other than the one which is laid, which is Jesus Christ. Now if any man builds upon the foundation with gold, silver, precious stones, wood, hay, straw, each man's work will become evident; for the day will show it, because it is to be revealed with fire; and the fire itself will test the quality of each man's work. If any man's work which he has built upon it remains, he shall receive a reward. If any man's work is burned up, he shall suffer loss; but he himself shall be saved, yet so as through fire.
>
> Do you not know that you are a temple of God, and that the Spirit of God dwells in you? If any man destroys the temple of God, God will destroy him, for the temple of God is holy, and that is what you are. (1 Cor. 3:10–17)

Take a look at your spiritual temple. Have you slipped off the foundation a little? Are your rafters sagging? Are you using gold, silver, and precious stones—or are you trying to get by with economy-grade wood, hay, and straw? How would you describe the state of your spiritual temple?

If things are starting to look kind of run-down, what do you think is at the root of the problem? Have you stopped working with a good contractor—"a wise master builder"—and gone the do-it-yourself route? Whose blueprints are you following for your life?

_____

_____

_____

Have you forgotten that the very Spirit of God dwells in you?
What do you need to do to make your life a fitting sanctuary for Him?

_____

_____

_____

Remember, *you* are the temple of the living God. Is your spiritual life any place to cut corners?

👑 *Living Insights*   STUDY TWO

Solomon's wide-ranging interest in the world around him wasn't
sinful or worldly-minded; instead, it honored the God who created
all of it. Sometimes, we Christians struggle with appreciating the
arts, exploring nature and the fascinations of science, and pursuing
higher learning. We can feel that it is somehow "secular" to show
an interest in the diversity of life surrounding us. If it isn't the Bible,
we don't want to "corrupt" ourselves with it.

In his award-winning book *Addicted to Mediocrity*, Franky
Schaeffer gives us a view of God that gently corrects this kind of
erroneous thinking. Read his words slowly and attentively; then
spend some time in prayer, asking God to give you a sense of the
freedom you have in Christ to enjoy His creation.

> If from this world around us we can learn any-
> thing about God's character, surely it is that we have
> a creative God, a God of diversity, a God whose
> interest in beauty and detail must be unquestioned
> when one looks at the world which he has made
> around us, and people themselves as the result of his
> craftsmanship.
> We could live in a flat uninteresting world, one

18

that had the bare minimum of gray ingredients to support life, one whose diversity was only enough to provide the minimum of existence. Instead, we live in a riotous explosion of diversity and beauty. We live in a world full of "useless" beauty, we live in a world of millions of species, we live in a world peopled by individuals of infinite variety, talents, abilities, and this is only on our own planet. When one looks heavenward and sees the complexity of the reaches of space above us, the mind boggles at the creativity of our God.[6]

6. Schaeffer, *Addicted to Mediocrity*, p. 17.

Chapter 3

SIGNS OF EROSION
Selected Scriptures

The Colorado River serpentines through the Arizona desert, taking little snaky licks along its path. It twists and turns through sandstone, limestone, shale, and granite, tirelessly slithering its way through the earth's strata. Laden with silt, the underbelly of the relentless river wears away the rock . . . grain by grain . . . pebble by pebble . . . day by day . . . year by year. The result? The Grand Canyon. More than half a million tons of sediment are eroded away each day from this gaping chasm.

Though the river is its main erosive agent, it is by no means the only one. Water flowing from short, violent rainstorms pushes sediment down slopes where there is little vegetation to impede it. Roots of trees and other plants burrowing into cracks pry the rocks loose, sending them crashing into the hungry river below. The chemical action of lichens eats away at the rocks they cling to. Water hiding in the hairline fissures of giant boulders freezes in the winter and chips away at their stony surfaces. Even the wind, with its blasts of airborne sand, pits away at the huge, gaping void of the canyon.

It's a monument now—that gash across the face of Arizona— a jagged testimony to the sweeping, destructive power of erosion.

Character, too, can erode like that, a grain of sand at a time . . . even character of granite, as polished as Solomon's.

A Flawless Image

Solomon stood exalted in the world as a towering, sculpted monument. There was no one as great, as wise, as rich, as envied.

The Blessing of God

As it was Michelangelo's touch that turned a block of stone into the exalted *Pietà*, so it was the touch of God that carved Solomon's place in history.

> Now Solomon the son of David established him-
> self securely over his kingdom, and the Lord his God

was with him and *exalted* him greatly. (2 Chron. 1:1, emphasis added)

The word *exalted* is from the Hebrew term *gadal*, which means to "grow up, become great or important, promote, make powerful . . . do great things."[1] The Amplified Bible renders this verse:

Solomon son of David was strengthened in his kingdom, and the Lord his God was with him and made him exceedingly great.

How great was he? Great enough that God gave him a blank-check opportunity to ask for whatever he wanted.

In that night God appeared to Solomon and said to him, "Ask what I shall give you." (verse 7)

And because of the purity of Solomon's request—wisdom and knowledge to rule God's people (vv. 8–10)—God gave "exceeding abundantly beyond all" that he asked or imagined (see Eph. 3:20).

And God said to Solomon, "Because you had this in mind, and did not ask for riches, wealth, or honor, or the life of those who hate you, nor have you even asked for long life, but you have asked for yourself wisdom and knowledge, that you may rule My people, over whom I have made you king, wisdom and knowledge have been granted to you. And I will give you riches and wealth and honor, such as none of the kings who were before you has possessed, nor those who will come after you." (vv. 11–12)

Solomon would be so blessed that he would be without peer: "There will not be any among the kings like you all your days" (1 Kings 3:13b).

A Variety of Interests

Like the glistening, snowcapped peak of Mount Everest, Solomon was the pinnacle of God's blessing on earth. His horizons of interest, as we studied in our previous chapter, were limitless—like the view from Everest (see 1 Kings 4:29–34). Therefore, when he fell, it was from great heights and over a wide territory.

1. *Theological Wordbook of the Old Testament*, ed. R. Laird Harris, Gleason L. Archer, Jr., Bruce K. Waltke (Chicago, Ill.: Moody Press, 1980), vol. 1, p. 151.

A Record of Achievements

In an unparalleled operation of cosmetic surgery, Solomon reconstructed the sagging face of Israel. For a duration of at least twenty years, Solomon smoothed the country's architectural wrinkles. Pools, houses, resorts, stables, fortresses, an exquisite home, and the breathtaking temple stood as tributes not only to his architectural and administrative skill but to his surgeon's patience as well (see 6:1, 38; 7:1; Eccles. 2:4–6).

The Praise of Men

A regular parade of fans pilgrimaged from the corners of the world to behold Solomon and all his glory (see 10:1, 6, 23–24). They gathered around his throne to pay him tribute, to pick his brain on difficult issues, to gather the pearls of wisdom that cascaded so fluidly from his lips. Fortune, fame, friends, and fulfilled fantasies became his daily delights. However, they soon became everyday, commonplace, so that he had to reach a little further, get just a bit more to maintain the "high" of his exalted position.

A Subtle Trap

In Solomon's diary, Ecclesiastes, the king's words orbit a constricted circle—the egocentric circle of self. The words *I* and *for myself* are a tiresome refrain whose repetition is broken only by the increasingly despairing verses of extravagance, boredom, and disillusionment.

Extravagance

In Ecclesiastes 2:1–8, Solomon records that he tried leisure, laughter, wine, work, possessions, and promiscuity; he experienced and amassed more and more until he sat back and said,

> Then I became great and increased more than all who preceded me in Jerusalem. My wisdom also stood by me. And all that my eyes desired I did not refuse them. I did not withhold my heart from any pleasure, for my heart was pleased because of all my labor and this was my reward for all my labor. (vv. 9–10)

Boredom

Surely all of that would satisfy the hungriest of souls . . . wouldn't it?

> Thus I considered all my activities which my hands
> had done and the labor which I had exerted, and
> behold all was vanity and striving after wind and
> there was no profit under the sun. (v. 11)

Sated yet empty, Solomon sighs,

> For there is no lasting remembrance of the wise man
> as with the fool, inasmuch as in the coming days all
> will be forgotten. And how the wise man and the
> fool alike die! So I hated life, for the work which
> had been done under the sun was grievous to me;
> because everything is futility and striving after wind.
> (vv. 16–17)

Disillusionment

From the boredom that comes with emptiness, that comes with
having lost touch with God and meaning, Solomon slid into the
deflation of disillusionment.

> Therefore I completely despaired of all the fruit of my
> labor for which I had labored under the sun. . . .
> For what does a man get in all his labor and in his
> striving with which he labors under the sun? Because
> all his days his task is painful and grievous; even
> at night his mind does not rest. This too is vanity.
> (vv. 20, 22–23)

A Deteriorating Life

From a distance, Solomon's exquisitely hewn character looms
impressive and striking. But a closer look reveals signs of erosion:
a chip here . . . a crack there . . . a compromise here . . . a
crumbling conviction there. However polished his granite character, Solomon—like all of us—had feet of clay. And those feet of
clay were slowly beginning to wash out beneath him.

Unwise Alliances with Unbelievers

The first sign of erosion we see in Solomon's character is a little
chip of compromise.

> Then Solomon formed a marriage alliance with Pha-
> raoh king of Egypt, and took Pharaoh's daughter and
> brought her to the city of David, until he had finished

building his own house and the house of the Lord and the wall around Jerusalem. (1 Kings 3:1; see also 7:8; 9:16, 24)

Solomon's marriage to Pharaoh's daughter was a union of two nations—not of two people. It was a marriage of expedience—not obedience to God's precepts. It was based on political diplomacy—not love. Furthermore, it was a compromise of God's Word.

In Deuteronomy 7:1–11, God laid down some very specific instructions to Israel regarding intermarriage with foreigners who worshiped other gods (see also Exod. 34:12–16; Ezra 9:1–3). Although we do see some conviction from Solomon on the matter (2 Chron. 8:11), his grip on God's Word shows definite signs of loosening.

Unholy Involvement with Idolatry

Erosion's second subtle sign comes with Solomon's continuance to worship on "the high places."

> The people were still sacrificing on the high places, because there was no house built for the name of the Lord until those days.
> Now Solomon loved the Lord, walking in the statutes of his father David, except he sacrificed and burned incense on the high places. (1 Kings 3:2–3)

Commentator Gene Rice explains the significance of these scenes.

> High places were local open air sanctuaries. Many had been taken over from the Canaanites and were open invitations to the seductive attraction of Canaanite cultic practice and ideology. The threat of Canaanite religion was not perceived at first, and the high places were regarded as acceptable places of worship by all, including Solomon. . . .
> . . . [However,] verses 1–3 imply that the seeds of the ignoble end of Solomon's reign were sown from the beginning. . . . [Verses 2–3] illustrate the kinds of rationalizations that make sin acceptable. Verse 2 uses the argument, "Everyone is doing it." Verse 3 creates the illusion that it is possible to love God and live a moral life and still "worship at the high places." Silently, invisibly, like an incubating

virus, sin was at work throughout Solomon's reign and in the end broke out in violent, destructive force.[2]

Unresolved Conflicts with Friends

In a business transaction with his friend Hiram, Solomon traded several cities in exchange for building materials. Hiram later inspected his newly acquired real estate and found he'd been cheated.

> And it came about at the end of twenty years in which Solomon had built the two houses, the house of the Lord and the king's house (Hiram king of Tyre had supplied Solomon with cedar and cypress timber and gold according to all his desire), then King Solomon gave Hiram twenty cities in the land of Galilee. So Hiram came out from Tyre to see the cities which Solomon had given him, and they did not please him. And he said, "What are these cities which you have given me, my brother?" So they were called the land of Cabul[3] to this day. (1 Kings 9:10–14)

Although he had been slighted, Hiram attempted to reconcile matters with Solomon (v. 14). However, Solomon made no effort to admit the wrong or to make things right. Again, we see signs of Solomon's character eroding in a shady business deal and ill-treatment of a friend.

Unrestrained Preoccupation with Sex

Solomon not only had Pharaoh's daughter as a wife, he indulged himself in a harem that was unequaled in the ancient Near East. It was his unrestrained preoccupation with sex that ultimately led him away from God.

> Now King Solomon loved many foreign women along with the daughter of Pharaoh: Moabite, Ammonite, Edomite, Sidonian, and Hittite women, from the nations concerning which the Lord had

---

2. Gene Rice, *Nations under God: A Commentary on the Book of 1 Kings,* International Theological Commentary series (Grand Rapids, Mich.: William B. Eerdmans Publishing Co., 1990), pp. 30–31. Those pagan altars of sacrifice were still operational in spite of God's command to "tear down their altars, and smash their sacred pillars, and hew down their Asherim, and burn their graven images with fire" (Deut. 7:5).

3. *Cabul* means "as good as nothing."

said to the sons of Israel, "You shall not associate with them, neither shall they associate with you, for they will surely turn your heart away after their gods." Solomon held fast to these in love. And he had seven hundred wives, princesses, and three hundred concubines, and his wives turned his heart away. (11:1–3)

Again, Solomon turned his head away from the clear teaching of God's Word (see Deut. 7:3–4). As a result, his seductive wives adulterated his heart.[4] As he flirted with sin, little by little the floodgates of an erosive stream were opening. Eventually, they would burst wide with a swollen river that would wash away the clay feet of Solomon's character.

A Strong Warning

This great, godly, gifted man, wisest of the wise, completely missed the torrent of destruction he was letting loose in his own life. Two streams in particular fed into the erosive current.

First, *he willfully ignored the counsel of Scripture.* He spent seven and a half years building a temple to house God's Word; the problem was, as soon as that house was built, he seemed content to let the Scriptures reside there rather than in his heart.

And second, *he had no accountability.* We never read of a prophet confronting Solomon. No, he was without peer, the single greatest person in the land. People were accountable to the king, not the other way around. Unfortunately, having no accountability ultimately spells disaster, no matter what your level in life.

As you ponder the shifting scenes in Solomon's story, take the lessons to heart and be on guard for the same signs of erosion in your life.

> Now these things happened to them as an example, and they were written for our instruction, upon whom the ends of the ages have come. Therefore let him who thinks he stands take heed lest he fall. (1 Cor. 10:11–12)

---

4. In the Old Testament, idolatry is viewed as spiritual prostitution and adultery (see Jer. 2:20–28; 3:6–9). Anything we give our hearts to that competes with our relationship with God and causes us to be unfaithful to Him is a form of idolatry.

Very few things deteriorate suddenly. No church suddenly splits. No child suddenly becomes delinquent. No friendship suddenly ends. No marriage suddenly dissolves. No building suddenly collapses. No Grand Canyon suddenly erodes. It happens slowly . . . grain by grain . . . compromise by compromise.

Do you see any erosion taking place in your life? Are you vulnerable in any of the same areas Solomon was?

_____

_____

_____

What are some of the signs you're seeing?

_____

_____

_____

How is this affecting your walk with the Lord? Are you wanting to pray less? Are you growing resistant to biblical counsel?

_____

_____

_____

What outcome of erosion is starting to form in your life?

_____

_____

_____

Perhaps it's time to start a soul conservation project and repair the foundations of your relationship with the Lord.

"Therefore everyone who hears these words of Mine, and acts upon them, may be compared to a wise man, who built his house upon the rock. And the rain descended, and the floods came, and the winds blew, and burst against that house; and yet it did not fall, for it had been founded upon the rock. And everyone who hears these words of Mine, and does not act upon them, will be like a foolish man, who built his house upon the sand. And the rain descended, and the floods came, and the winds blew, and burst against that house; and it fell, and great was its fall." (Matt. 7:24–27)

If the erosion isn't stopped, the rains of life's storms will wash you away. Won't you come before God now in a spirit of confession, asking Him to help you want to build your life "upon the rock"? He is faithful both to forgive and to establish, desiring you to be on safe, solid ground in your relationship with Him.

And now, little children, abide in Him, so that when He appears, we may have confidence and not shrink away from Him in shame at His coming. (1 John 2:28)

⚜ *Living Insights*

Solomon's glory soon began to lose its luster. Earthly pleasures have a way of doing that, as the poet Robert Burns noted:

But pleasures are like poppies spread:
You seize the flow'r, its bloom is shed;
Or like the snow falls in the river,
A moment white—then melts for ever.[5]

Then what does last?

All flesh is grass, and all its loveliness is like the
flower of the field. . . .
The grass withers, the flower fades,
But the word of our God stands forever.
(Isa. 40:6b, 8)

---

5. Robert Burns, in *The Home Book of Quotations: Classical and Modern*, 10th ed., comp. Burton Stevenson (1967; reprint, New York, N.Y.: Dodd, Mead and Co., 1984), p. 1512.

His Word is what lasts. A lot of what busies us will eventually fade and melt away. Only His Word *really* lasts.

Are you investing enough of your time in God's Word? Enough of your life? If you'd like to but don't know where to begin, the *One Year Bible* is a good place to start. Or try going through the shorter epistles, one each week. Whatever you decide, the important thing is to do it! Because only His Word and presence can keep your character from eroding (see Ps. 119:9, 11).

Chapter 4

WHEN THE HEART IS TURNED AWAY

1 Kings 11:1–9

It doesn't take a lot to wreck a brand-new automobile—too much to drink . . . too much daydreaming . . . too much nodding off at the wheel. Self-indulgence at the wrong time or in the wrong amount can lead to disaster, whether you're driving a car or directing a kingdom.

Cruising behind the wheel of a head-turning kingdom, Solomon had a heavy foot on the accelerator. His spiritual eyelids, though, were growing heavy. Intoxicated with fame, fortune, and females, he would need more than black coffee to sober up to his responsibilities as ruler of God's people. With only one arm propped on the steering wheel of the kingdom, Solomon was fast on his way to becoming a spiritual fatality.

Analysis of Tangible Success

Like a teenager on a Friday night date in his father's new sports car, Solomon appeared to have it all. He had an incredible fortune (1 Kings 10:14–25), widespread fame (vv. 23–25), unlimited power (4:21–25), and innumerable pleasures (Eccles. 2:1–10). He had a marvelous heritage, good training at the feet of Nathan the prophet, and a heart that beat strong and sincere for God. Although a young ruler in the driver's seat of a powerful kingdom, Solomon had been given the keys with both God's and his father's blessing (1 Chron. 28:5). And in that driver's seat he sat tall and proud and "became greater than all the kings of the earth in riches and in wisdom" (1 Kings 10:23).

So what, then, broke down? What came loose? What went out of alignment?

Characteristics of Personal Deterioration

The problem in Solomon's life appears to have been a slow leak in his relationship with God. A pinprick leak, unattended, is all it took. Day by day a little spiritual air seeped out of Solomon's life, until one morning he woke up and found his relationship with God flat.

Internal Attitudes

Two sharp slivers slowly penetrated Solomon's walk with God: failing to take God seriously and failing to be accountable. We touched on these in our previous lesson; let's look at them in more detail now.

1. *Failing to take God seriously.* Solomon tolerated what God condemned and embraced what God abhorred. By doing so, he failed to take God at His word.

> Then Solomon formed a marriage alliance with Pharaoh king of Egypt, and took Pharaoh's daughter and brought her to the city of David, until he had finished building his own house and the house of the Lord and the wall around Jerusalem. (1 Kings 3:1)

Throughout the writings of Moses, Joshua, and Samuel, God had warned against this practice of marrying foreign women.[1] But Solomon didn't take it seriously. In the parallel book of 2 Chronicles, we see more evidence of Solomon's wavering commitment toward God's Law.

> Then Solomon brought Pharaoh's daughter up from the city of David to the house which he had built for her; for he said, "My wife shall not dwell in the house of David king of Israel, because the places are holy where the ark of the Lord has entered." (8:11)

Apparently, Solomon had brought his Egyptian bride to the city of David and kept her there under wraps, hidden behind the scenes so as not to attract too much attention. To Solomon's credit, we do see some conviction in his life—he protected the sacredness of Israel's holy things. His relationship with God, then, was not yet totally flat.

But the sliver was there nevertheless: he had built a house just for her. Solomon knew that a woman with an unholy lifestyle had no business being in a holy place. But to his discredit, he found a place for her, built a house for her, and undoubtedly spent much time there with her himself. By ensconcing her in his kingdom and in his heart, he was subtly inviting in a world of idolatry, infidelity,

---

1. See Exodus 34:11–16; Deuteronomy 7:3–4; Joshua 23:11–13; Judges 3:4–7.

and innumerable other iniquities.

How could he knowingly choose something so obviously wrong? And how can *we*? For if we're honest, we have to admit that sometimes we are as willful as Solomon. And, like overinflated tires, many of us also have internal pressures that make us more vulnerable to a spiritual blowout.

First, we can become *overexposed* to the things of God—which leads to cynicism. Constantly rubbing up against spiritual things often results not in tenderness but in callousness, gradually causing us to lose our sensitivity toward God, as Solomon did.

Second, we can get *overindulged*, given too much for nothing—which leads to irresponsibility. David did the fighting while Solomon reveled in the benefits. Likewise, parents can hand over an already successful business that's had all the struggles worked out or pass down a lifestyle that took a lifetime to earn, and children can easily take it all for granted.

Third, we can be *overpromoted*, go too far too fast—which leads to sterile professionalism. We miss many of the essential growing pains and pleasures of the upward climb on the professional ladder when we zoom right to an inexperienced top.

Have you been overexposed? Overindulged? Overpromoted? Are you doing this to your children . . . the people you work with . . . the church? Remember: Overinflated tires wear out faster and are more susceptible to blowouts.

2. Failing to be accountable. The second sliver puncturing Solomon's spiritual life is his lack of accountability. Alone in the driver's seat of the kingdom, Solomon answered to no one. The words "all that Solomon desired to do" (1 Kings 9:1b) and "all that it pleased Solomon to build" (v. 19b; 2 Chron. 8:6b) reflected the absolute nature of his rule. He acquired vast riches and constructed sprawling storage cities to secure them. He also built elaborate centers for his horses, horsemen, and chariots.

> So Solomon rebuilt Gezer and the lower Beth-horon and Baalath and Tamar in the wilderness, in the land of Judah, and all the storage cities which Solomon had, even the cities for his chariots and the cities for his horsemen, and all that it pleased Solomon to build in Jerusalem, in Lebanon, and in all the land under his rule. (1 Kings 9:17–19)

Whatever "pleased Solomon" he did. Whatever he desired,

longed for, coveted was his. This unaccountability was passed on to his son Rehoboam, who ruled according to his capricious desires and catastrophically "forsook the counsel of the elders" (2 Chron. 10:6–8).[2]

However, there was One to whom Solomon was accountable, whether he acknowledged it or not. And that Almighty One was soon going to call His errant king to account—personally.

Lord's Appearances

God visited Solomon on three specific occasions. The first encounter was at the inception of his reign, and it was one of the most beautiful meetings in all the Scriptures (1 Kings 3:5–14). God told Solomon in a dream: "Ask what you wish Me to give you" (v. 5). Solomon responded with a purely motivated request for "an understanding heart to judge Thy people to discern between good and evil" (v. 9). And God granted his wish but added a postscripted condition to His promise.

> "If you walk in My ways, keeping My statutes and commandments, as your father David walked, then I will prolong your days." (v. 14)

The second encounter is found in 1 Kings 9:1–9. This time, however, a strong tone of caution tinges God's words.

> "And as for you, if you will walk before Me as your father David walked, in integrity of heart and uprightness, doing according to all that I have commanded you and will keep My statutes and My ordinances, then I will establish the throne of your kingdom over Israel forever, just as I promised to your father David, saying, 'You shall not lack a man on the throne of Israel.' But if you or your sons shall indeed turn away from following Me, and shall not keep My commandments and My statutes which I have set before you and shall go and serve other gods and worship them, then I will cut off Israel from the land which I have given them, and the

---

2. Compare the heritage Solomon laid up for Rehoboam with the legacy God instructed Israel's kings to pass on in Deuteronomy 17:18–20. Verses 18–19 specifically address how the king was supposed to keep his heart sensitive to God, and verse 20 spells out the need for accountability: "that [the king's] heart may not be lifted up above his countrymen."

house which I have consecrated for My name, I will cast out of My sight. So Israel will become a proverb and a byword among all peoples. And this house will become a heap of ruins; everyone who passes by will be astonished and hiss and say, 'Why has the Lord done thus to this land and to this house?' And they will say, 'Because they forsook the Lord their God, who brought their fathers out of the land of Egypt, and adopted other gods and worshiped them and served them, therefore the Lord has brought all this adversity on them.'" (vv. 4–9)

God sees the leak in Solomon's life and is warning him to patch it before he destroys the kingdom.

The third encounter occurs in 1 Kings 11. This time, the tone is castigatory. God is angry—and for good reason. Power has corrupted the pure heart of the throne.

Final Steps of Failure

The backdrop to God's anger in 1 Kings 11 is found in Deuteronomy 17:14–17, where the job description for Israel's kings is on file.

"When you enter the land which the Lord your God gives you, and you possess it and live in it, and you say, 'I will set a king over me like all the nations who are around me,' you shall surely set a king over you whom the Lord your God chooses, one from among your countrymen you shall set as king over yourselves; you may not put a foreigner over yourselves who is not your countryman. Moreover, he shall not multiply horses for himself, nor shall he cause the people to return to Egypt to multiply horses, since the Lord has said to you, 'You shall never again return that way.' Neither shall he multiply wives for himself, lest his heart turn away; nor shall he greatly increase silver and gold for himself."

In the course of his lengthy reign, Solomon violated almost every one of God's stipulations: he not only multiplied horses for himself, but he went as far as Egypt to acquire them; and he multiplied wives for himself, as well as gold and silver. Turning now to 1 Kings 11, we see the bellows that inflamed God's wrath.

34

Step One: Solomon Willfully Ignored God's Written Word

> Now King Solomon loved many foreign women along with the daughter of Pharaoh: Moabite, Ammonite, Edomite, Sidonian, and Hittite women, from the nations concerning which the Lord had said to the sons of Israel, "You shall not associate with them, neither shall they associate with you, for they will surely turn your heart away after their gods." (vv. 1–2a)

How far Solomon had fallen from those first pure days of prayer and sacrifice at the beginning of his reign! Pleasing himself rather than pleasing the God who had given him everything had become his tragic first priority.

Step Two: Solomon Flaunted His Own Desires

> Solomon held fast to these in love. And he had seven hundred wives, princesses, and three hundred concubines, and his wives turned his heart away. (vv. 2b–3)

Not content to cling to one foreign lover, or ten, or even a hundred, Solomon gathered a thousand and flaunted them in God's face.

Step Three: Solomon Resisted Being Totally Committed to the Things of God

> For it came about when Solomon was old, his wives turned his heart away after other gods; and his heart was not wholly devoted to the Lord his God, as the heart of David his father had been. . . . And Solomon did what was evil in the sight of the Lord, and did not follow the Lord fully, as David his father had done. (vv. 4, 6)

Now a slave to his lusts and the women who sated them, Solomon descended into the darkness of a divided heart and the unspeakable shame of spiritual adultery.

Step Four: Solomon Pursued the Satisfaction of Ungodly Companions

> For Solomon went after Ashtoreth the goddess of

the Sidonians and after Milcom the detestable idol of the Ammonites. . . . Then Solomon built a high place for Chemosh the detestable idol of Moab, on the mountain which is east of Jerusalem, and for Molech the detestable idol of the sons of Ammon. Thus also he did for all his foreign wives, who burned incense and sacrificed to their gods.[3] (vv. 5, 7–8)

In the verses that follow, we feel the heat and see the flame in God's eyes as He speaks to Solomon.

Now the Lord was angry with Solomon because his heart was turned away from the Lord, the God of Israel, who had appeared to him twice, and had commanded him concerning this thing, that he should not go after other gods; but he did not observe what the Lord had commanded. So the Lord said to Solomon, "Because you have done this, and you have not kept My covenant and My statutes, which I have commanded you, I will surely tear the kingdom from you, and will give it to your servant." (vv. 9–11)

A Concluding Application

As Solomon's life recklessly careens by, the dust settles around two messages billboarded by the side of the road. First, *no heart is suddenly turned away*. Dissipation doesn't come in a day; it is the result of a life course of destructive choices. But the good news is: *no one who has slipped needs to stay in that condition*. God tried to get Solomon's attention twice, remember. If your heart has turned away and you want to turn it back, take hold of God's outstretched hand, won't you?

If we confess our sins, He is faithful and righteous to forgive us our sins and to cleanse us from all unrighteousness. (1 John 1:9)

---

3. Ashtoreth was the goddess of love, maternity, and fertility. Milcom was the Ammonite god of authority. Chemosh and Molech were gods whose rituals included child sacrifice. It's interesting to note that when the heart is turned away, the three characteristics of these gods—sensuality, stubborn pride, and cruelty—are often present.

Our gracious God is a God of fresh starts, as Solomon's father, David, knew from experience:

> For as high as the heavens are above the earth,
> So great is His lovingkindness toward those who fear
> Him.
> As far as the east is from the west,
> So far has He removed our transgressions from us.
> Just as a father has compassion on his children,
> So the Lord has compassion on those who fear Him.
> (Ps. 103:11–13)

Living Insights STUDY ONE

First Kings 11 reads like a tragic accident report of a drunken driver. Too much indulgence; too little resistance. Too much power; too little restraint. At first, the joyride is filled with thrills and laughter. But notice how Solomon's tires gradually drift into the oncoming lane:

- "Now King Solomon loved many foreign women" (v. 1)

- "and his wives turned his heart away" (v. 3)

- "his wives turned his heart away after other gods; and his heart was not wholly devoted to the Lord his God, as the heart of David his father had been" (v. 4)

- "and Solomon did what was evil in the sight of the Lord" (v. 6)

In a drunken stupor of self-indulgence, Solomon skids around the hairpin turns of promiscuity and idolatry, speeding through the dark with his headlights off. As a result, God does what any good friend would do: He grabs the steering wheel, hits the brakes, and takes away the keys (v. 11).

May I talk to you briefly, as a friend? Are the tires of your life drifting into some wrong lanes? Are you beginning to skid into the oncoming traffic of God's judgment? If so, please, *please* pull over. Put yourself in the hands of someone who cares, and let that friend drive you home, back to Jesus, where you belong—before you become another grim highway statistic.

Most of us are familiar with the basic Christian teachings about accountability. Children should be accountable to parents; wives, to husbands; husbands, to Christ; laypeople, to elders; citizens, to government; one, to another, and so forth.

However, the New Testament shows us a more refined sense of accountability than perhaps many of us are aware of. Husbands are directed to love their wives in a sacrificial and sensitive way (Eph. 5:25; 1 Pet. 3:7), fathers are to deal tenderly with their children (Eph. 6:4), and elders are commissioned to be shepherds of their flock, not lords (1 Pet. 5:1–3).

The key to *all* these relationships is submission—servanthood that flows out of humility, honor, and love for one another.

How accountable are you to others? Are you humble enough to admit that you sometimes need help staying on track?

_____

_____

Does the idea of accountability feel threatening to you? Why?

_____

_____

_____

If you had several wise, trusted, and godly people in your life to whom you could be accountable—people who were sensitive, servantlike, shepherdlike, and sacrificial—would that make a difference in your attitude toward this concept? If you know anybody like that, jot down their names.

_____

_____

_____

On the flip side, how sensitive, servantlike, shepherdlike, and sacrificial are you to those who are accountable to you?

_____

_____

_____

Remember, being accountable doesn't mean being controlled or dominated by another person. The goal and purpose of it is to help you keep walking "in a manner worthy of the God who calls you into His own kingdom and glory" (1 Thess. 2:12). That, and that alone, is the guiding principle behind accountability.

Chapter 5

HOW GOD DEALS WITH DEFIANCE

1 Kings 11:9–28, 40

In the long season of his reign, Solomon sowed a lot of chaff to the wind, a lot of empty husks of self-indulgence. It is no wonder he came to the conclusion that so much of his life was vanity . . . emptiness . . . striving after the wind (Eccles. 2:10–11). It is also no surprise that Solomon would eventually harvest what he sowed.

> "For they sow the wind,
> And they reap the whirlwind." (Hos. 8:7a)

Solomon had sown the winds of wickedness, and on the horizon was the whirlwind of God's wrath.[1]

> A jealous and avenging God is the Lord;
> The Lord is avenging and wrathful.
> The Lord takes vengeance on His adversaries,
> And He reserves wrath for His enemies.
> The Lord is slow to anger and great in power,
> And the Lord will by no means leave the guilty
> unpunished.
> In whirlwind and storm is His way,
> And clouds are the dust beneath His feet.
> (Nah. 1:2–3)

In 1 Kings 11 the storm clouds of God's impending judgment are gathering, stirred by Solomon's involvement with idolatry (vv. 1–8). However, it is Solomon's defiance in the face of God's rebuke that will whip the winds into a holy fury. Ironically, Solomon's own counsel about defiance returned later in his life to indict him.

> "Because I called, and you refused;
> I stretched out my hand, and no one paid
> attention;
> And you neglected all my counsel,

---

1. In the Old Testament, one of the images associated with God's judgment is the whirlwind (see Ps. 58:9; Prov. 10:25).

And did not want my reproof;
I will laugh at your calamity;
I will mock when your dread comes,
When your dread comes like a storm,
And your calamity comes on like a whirlwind."
(Prov. 1:24–27a)

Defiance: Seeds and Harvest

At the heart of the fierce blasts of judgment is a heart brimming with rebellion. Romans 1:28–32 starkly delineates the nature of a rebellious, defiant person.

> And just as they did not see fit to acknowledge God any longer, God gave them over to a depraved mind, to do those things which are not proper, being filled with all unrighteousness, wickedness, greed, evil; full of envy, murder, strife, deceit, malice; they are gossips, slanderers, haters of God, insolent, arrogant, boastful, inventors of evil, disobedient to parents, without understanding, untrustworthy, unloving, unmerciful; and although they know the ordinance of God, that those who practice such things are worthy of death, they not only do the same, but also give hearty approval to those who practice them.

In God's eyes, the inward spirit of rebellion is as evil as the outward action of idolatry: "For rebellion is as bad as the sin of witchcraft, and stubbornness is as bad as worshiping idols" (1 Sam. 15:23a LB). So dangerous is the character trait of defiance that extreme measures were instituted in Israel's legal system to protect the community from its malignant spread.

> "If any man has a stubborn and rebellious son who will not obey his father or his mother, and when they chastise him, he will not even listen to them, then his father and mother shall seize him, and bring him out to the elders of his city at the gateway of his home town. And they shall say to the elders of his city, 'This son of ours is stubborn and rebellious, he will not obey us, he is a glutton and a drunkard.' Then all the men of his city shall stone him to death; so you shall remove the evil from your midst, and

all Israel shall hear of it and fear." (Deut. 21:18–21)

In Solomon we find a stubborn, rebellious, defiant man; not a young man still living at home, as in Deuteronomy 21, but an adult of at least forty-five years of age. And not just any man but the richest man in all the world, the son of David, the king of Israel.

The seeds he threw to the wind were compromise, which harvested him a loss of distinctiveness as king of a nation set apart; extravagance, which brought forth boredom and disillusionment; unaccountability, from which sprouted unchecked independence; and idolatry, which yielded lust and open defiance. Two times in 1 Kings 11 we are told that his heart was turned away from God (vv. 4, 9). Consequently, because Solomon would not turn to God, God turned to him—in anger.

Reaction: God and Solomon

Because God is slow to anger and infinitely compassionate (Ps. 103:8), we could easily be lulled into believing that He is soft and tolerant of sin. But being slow to anger does not mean never being angry. Sin is not tolerable to Him. And when warnings and reproofs are spurned, His judgment comes upon us like a whirlwind and His anger, like a fire (Deut. 4:24; Ps. 90:7).[2]

Divine Anger

His wrath kindling, God ignites the tinders of judgment under the defiant king.

> Now the Lord was angry with Solomon because his heart was turned away from the Lord, the God of Israel, who had appeared to him twice, and had commanded him concerning this thing, that he should not go after other gods; but he did not observe what the Lord had commanded. So the Lord said to Solomon, "Because you have done this, and you have not kept My covenant and My statutes, which I have commanded you, I will surely tear the kingdom from you, and will give it to your servant. Nevertheless I will not do it in your days for the

---

2. The word *charah*, translated "to burn with anger" or "to be kindled with anger," carries with it the idea of kindling a fire or the heat of the anger once kindled. Compare Numbers 11:33, 12:9 and Psalms 69:24, 74:1.

sake of your father David, but I will tear it out of the hand of your son. However, I will not tear away all the kingdom, but I will give one tribe to your son for the sake of My servant David and for the sake of Jerusalem which I have chosen." (1 Kings 11:9–13)

Three times in these verses God uses the fearsome word *tear*. God's judgment is a tearing experience, a ripping away of that which means so much to us. It leaves our peace in pieces and our relationships in jagged tatters. It is strong and hard, severe and heartwrenching. And it was the only way left to get through to Solomon.

Yet, with the word *nevertheless* in verse 12, God's mercy pierces radiantly earthward through the ominous clouds of judgment that hover on Solomon's horizon. Because of God's love for David and for Jerusalem, He will mercifully hold back the turbulent times of civil war until after Solomon's death.

Human Adversaries

At first glance, it appears that Solomon got off easy—all the bad times for the kingdom would happen when he was no longer around. The guilt of bringing hardship and ruin to the future of God's people might have haunted someone whose heart was still soft toward God and the meaning in life, but it would most likely fade into an unfeelable distance in a heart hardened by defiance. So, to keep His judgment inescapably near to Solomon, God moved in on an area the king had taken for granted.

So far, Solomon had known only peace in his reign. But now God was calling His hounds to begin nipping at the heels of Solomon's royal sandals.

> Then the Lord raised up an adversary to Solomon, Hadad the Edomite; he was of the royal line in Edom. (v. 14)

The first of Solomon's adversaries was Hadad the Edomite (vv. 14–22). Years before, this young prince narrowly managed to escape a massacre at the hands of David's army (vv. 15–17). He fled to Egypt, where he "found great favor before Pharaoh" (v. 19). Later, he married Pharaoh's sister-in-law, who bore him a son who grew up with the ruler's own children (vv. 19–20). In the years that followed, however, neither the pleasures nor power of Pharaoh's palace could erase the scars Hadad had suffered from David.

> But when Hadad heard in Egypt that David slept
> with his fathers, and that Joab the commander of
> the army was dead, Hadad said to Pharaoh, "Send
> me away, that I may go to my own country." Then
> Pharaoh said to him, "But what have you lacked
> with me, that behold, you are seeking to go to your
> own country?" And he answered, "Nothing; never-
> theless you must surely let me go." (vv. 21–22)

Clearly, Hadad was hot on the trail of revenge—a trail that led
straight to David's heir, Solomon.

Meanwhile, Rezon from Damascus, a wild dog from a different
pack, was also picking up Solomon's scent.

> God also raised up another adversary to him,
> Rezon the son of Eliada, who had fled from his lord
> Hadadezer king of Zobah. And he gathered men to
> himself and became leader of a marauding band,
> after David slew them of Zobah; and they went to
> Damascus and stayed there, and reigned in Damascus.
> So he was an adversary to Israel all the days of
> Solomon, along with the evil that Hadad did; and he
> abhorred Israel and reigned over Aram. (vv. 23–25)

Internal Rebellion

Hadad and Rezon, from Egypt and Damascus, were external
threats to the kingdom. However, internal unrest also began to
gnaw at Solomon's reign, as one of Solomon's most trusted men—
Jeroboam—rebelled against his king.

> Then Jeroboam the son of Nebat, an Ephraimite of
> Zeredah, Solomon's servant, whose mother's name was
> Zeruah, a widow, also rebelled against the king. (v. 26)

Jeroboam was a "valiant warrior" and "industrious," appointed
by Solomon to oversee the forced labor for the house of Joseph (v.
28). He was so trusted by Solomon that only the intervention of
God could drive a wedge between them—which is exactly what
happened. In verses 29–39, God speaks to Jeroboam through His
prophet Ahijah, informing him of Solomon's idolatry and defiance
and of His plan to divide the kingdom and give part to Jeroboam.

> "'But I will take the kingdom from his son's hand

and give it to you, even ten tribes. . . . And I will take you, and you shall reign over whatever you desire, and you shall be king over Israel.'" (vv. 35, 37)

Personal Frustration

As if the presence of his adversaries wasn't enough, Solomon encounters immense personal frustration as well.

Solomon sought therefore to put Jeroboam to death; but Jeroboam arose and fled to Egypt to Shishak king of Egypt, and he was in Egypt until the death of Solomon. (v. 40)

Solomon was one of the richest, most powerful men in the world. He was king, yet he felt as helpless as a pawn with regard to Jeroboam. Like a chess piece craftily eluding capture, Jeroboam slipped between Solomon's fingers—to wait in the protected square of Egypt until the time was ripe to move in and checkmate the king.

The Downward Steps of Defiance

Solomon could have penned these words of the poet Byron:

The thorns which I have reap'd are of the tree
I planted,—they have torn me—and I bleed:
I should have known what fruit would spring from
such a seed.[3]

Solomon should have known, but even wisdom can't always protect us from the darkness of our hearts. To help prevent us from being torn and bleeding, we need to remember three truths about defiance.

First, *defiance begins with carnal attitudes*. It's like a staircase leading to the very basement of spiritual experience, with each steep step taking us dizzily downward:

SELFISHNESS: "I want my own way."

STUBBORNNESS: "I won't quit until I get it."

INDIFFERENCE: "I don't care who it hurts."

---

3. Lord Byron, *Childe Harold's Pilgrimage*, canto 4, stanza 10, in *The Complete Poetical Works of Byron* (Boston, Mass.: Houghton Mifflin Co., 1933), p. 56.

RESISTANCE: "I refuse to listen to counsel."

CONTEMPT: "I am not concerned about the consequences."

You can almost hear the crash in the dark at the bottom of the stairs, can't you?

Second, *defiance leads to personal misery.* Solomon's own words in Proverbs 13:15 alert us that "the way of the treacherous is hard." The treacherous or faithless person—the person who has descended the steps of selfishness, indifference, and contempt—travels a way that is "hard." The word translated *hard* carries with it the ideas "perennial, everflowing, permanent, enduring," like "the perennial running water in a stream."[4] In this context it means "lack of faith forms its own rut from which there is no escape."[5] A miserable existence indeed.

And last, *defiance results in inescapable bondage.* Once again we turn to the testimony of Solomon.

> His own iniquities will capture the wicked,
> And he will be held with the cords of his sin.
> (Prov. 5:22)

Freedom is not to be found in defiance; it is only found in the One who sets the captives free (Luke 4:18). Jesus Himself said,

> "I came that they might have life, and might have it abundantly." (John 10:10b)

Don't cheat yourself with the illusory pleasures of defiance, as Solomon did. Instead, set your heart toward God and on the everlasting riches of life in Him.

Living Insights

When we seek to elude God by walking down the dark streets of defiance, He has ways of calling dogs from all sorts of alleys. Often we don't even know they're there. They just sort of skulk in the

---

4. *Theological Wordbook of the Old Testament,* ed. R. Laird Harris, Gleason L. Archer, Jr., Bruce K. Waltke (Chicago, Ill.: Moody Press, 1980), vol. 1, p. 419.

5. *Theological Wordbook of the Old Testament,* p. 419.

shadows—until God whistles. Then, like bloodhounds, they're off and running, hot on the scent. Baying and barking, they sniff us out wherever we may be hiding. Tenacious. Tireless. At times, terrifying.

These wild dogs may take the form of a memory . . . a face from the past . . . a bankruptcy . . . an illness. When David kept silent about his sin with Bathsheba and the murder of Uriah, God loosed His hounds:

> For day and night Thy hand was heavy upon me;
> My vitality was drained away as with the fever
> heat of summer. (Ps. 32:4)

Are you one of His children skipping footloose and defiant through life? Are you letting your heart be turned away, turned off to God? Even the smallest seed can grow and spread into an unmanageable, tangled crop. If you detect even a hint of defiance, bring it out into the light by writing down your situation. (If you've been through a time of defiance and come out on the other side of God's dealing with you, use this Living Insights as an opportunity to write down what you learned. Just transfer these present questions into a past situation.)

What part of God's Word are you knowingly violating? What is His warning for doing so?

Does the possibility of judgment seem remote, perhaps at a safe distance? Why do you feel this way?

Look into the secret places of your heart, and try to answer why you are choosing a defiant path.

_____

_____

_____

_____

Wouldn't it be better to address honestly whatever hurt or frustration is driving you on than to sow defiance and reap a harvest of destruction? Than to desperately try to outrun the hounds of God? God is faithful to forgive *and* to guide. Won't you turn to Him again and let Him show you the way out of the dark, dangerous alleys and into a way of purity and peace instead (compare Gal. 6:7–8)?

👑 *Living Insights* 　　　　　　　　　　　　STUDY TWO

Are you vulnerable to any of the five carnal attitudes that mark a person's descent into defiance? To help protect yourself from a painful stumble down that steep staircase, let the following questions act as a lamp to your feet and a light to your path.

What influences in your life foster the "I want my own way" syndrome? How have you noticed their effects on you?

_____

_____

_____

In what subtle ways do you manifest the stubborn "I won't quit until I get it" attitude?

_____

_____

_____

Many times, indifference toward the well-being of others has its root in indifference toward our own well-being. What prompts that indifferent attitude toward yourself so that you say, "I don't care who it hurts—even if it's me"?

_____

_____

_____

How do you quietly get around listening to the counsel of others?

_____

_____

_____

Can you think of occasions in your life or in the lives of those you know when defiance hasn't led to personal misery? Expand on that.

_____

_____

_____

Have you ever become the victim of something you pursued? How did that come about?

_____

_____

_____

If the light of these questions has illuminated some shadowy vulnerabilities toward defiance, what will you do to prevent yourself from stumbling in the dark?

_____

_____

_____

_____

SOUND ADVICE FROM AN OLD REBEL
Ecclesiastes 11:9–12:7

O steoporosis . . . arthritis . . . arteriosclerosis . . . angina. Cold, sterile medical terms with Latin roots and antiseptic sounds; diseases of the elderly. Sadly, the autumn years of most lives are not a treeful of fall's flaming colors. Rather, they are scattered shreds of brittleness that crunch dryly under life's heavy footsteps. Memories, often muted with regret, cluster in little wind-blown piles—"If only time could be turned back. . . . If only I had it to do all over again. . . . If only . . ."

Perhaps the hardest thing to face about old age is not the physical pain, but the guilt connected with feelings of wasted days spent in waywardness and rebellion.

Such is the case of Solomon in his old age. Like arthritis rusting away his joints, remorse for his former life creaked from deep inside and made every bone ache. Painfully stiff and inflamed, his autumn days were anything but golden.

Solomon's Closing Years

As the sun westered away on Solomon's life, the self-indulgent pleasures of his earlier years thinned on the horizon. All that remained was the burning memory of his infidelity to God. As brutal reminders of his defiant days, three God-positioned enemies cast long shadows across Solomon's deathbed—Hadad from Edom, Rezon from Damascus, and Jeroboam from Israel.

Although his forty-year reign was a golden age of peace for Israel, as the sun set on his life, the foreboding clouds of judgment were gathering in turbulent clusters and closing in on him.

Solomon's Advice to the Young

In Ecclesiastes, the diary of his latter years, Solomon records his regrets and his advice to younger readers.

Remember—You Are Accountable to God

Characteristically, many lose their sense of physical balance as they grow older. Oftentimes, however, as in the case of Solomon, spiritual balance becomes keener.

> Rejoice, young man, during your childhood, and let your heart be pleasant during the days of young manhood. And follow the impulses of your heart and the desires of your eyes. Yet know that God will bring you to judgment for all these things. (Eccles. 11:9)

The heat of youth's passion is to be tempered with the reality that all of our actions will one day be placed on the unyielding anvil of God's judgment. Consequently, the fleeting prime of our life should be weighed against the permanence of eternity.

> So, remove vexation from your heart and put away pain from your body, because childhood and the prime of life are fleeting. (11:10)

The Hebrew word for *vexation* means to "agitate, stir up, or provoke the heart to a heated condition. . . . The term when applied to God, implies that man can affect the very heart of God so as to cause him heat, pain, or grief."[1] Get rid of those things that break the heart of God—this is Solomon's counsel to us—and invest your energies in doing what pleases Him.

Get Your Priorities on Target Early

Most people tend to put off any kind of commitment until later in life—"I'll wait till I've had my fling with life, wait till I get older and settle down, then I'll look into spiritual things a little more." Solomon advises just the opposite.

> Remember also your Creator in the days of your youth, before the evil days come and the years draw near when you will say, "I have no delight in them." (12:1)

What does it mean to "remember also your Creator"? It is to determinedly include Him in your day-to-day life. It is to work,

---

1. *Theological Wordbook of the Old Testament*, ed. R. Laird Harris, Gleason L. Archer, Jr., Bruce K. Waltke (Chicago, Ill.: Moody Press, 1980), vol. 1, p. 451.

acknowledging Him as both partner and patron of your business (Col. 3:23). It is to make decisions, consulting Him for direction and approval.

To remember your Creator is to realize that all good things in life are handcrafted gifts from God (see James 1:17)—every physical blessing, every spiritual blessing, every step, every breath (Acts 17:28). God is the key to everything in life that really matters: every relationship, every struggle, every decision.

Making a conscious, purposeful effort to remember Him now is the only way we'll be able to one day look back over our years and say, "I have delight in them!"

Age Works against You, Not for You

In a vividly poetic way, Solomon describes the stark realities of aging. They are days of darkness and clouds, of weakness and idleness, of poor hearing and light sleeping.

> Before the sun, the light, the moon, and the stars are darkened, and clouds return after the rain; in the day that the watchmen of the house tremble, and mighty men stoop, the grinding ones stand idle because they are few, and those who look through windows grow dim; and the doors on the street are shut as the sound of the grinding mill is low, and one will arise at the sound of the bird, and all the daughters of song will sing softly.[2] (Eccles. 12:2–4)

Solomon's tone becomes even more sober as he continues his dirge on the plight of the elderly. Fear, impotence, and separation from loved ones are the low notes of old age.

> Furthermore, men are afraid of a high place and of terrors on the road; the almond tree blossoms, the grasshopper drags himself along, and the caperberry is ineffective. For man goes to his eternal home while mourners go about in the street. (v. 5)

We don't get stronger when we get older . . . we get weaker.

---

2. The "watchman of the house" would be the trembling lips of the old person; the "mighty men" are the legs and back; the "grinding ones" are the teeth; "those who look through windows" are the eyes; the shut doors and low "sound of the grinding mill" represent loss of hearing; and arising at the slightest sound of a bird shows the inability to sleep soundly.

So if we wait until old age to get our life straight with God, we may very well not have the strength to do it.

Death Is Inevitable—Sooner than Many Think

As if from his deathbed, pulling himself up to utter his last words, Solomon looks us straight in the eye and pleads:

> Remember Him before the silver cord is broken and
> the golden bowl is crushed, the pitcher by the well
> is shattered and the wheel at the cistern is crushed;
> then the dust will return to the earth as it was, and
> the spirit will return to God who gave it. (vv. 6–7)

Like an earthenware pitcher that falls to the ground and shatters, spilling its water to evaporate into the air, so when we die, our broken bodies will return to the earth and our spirits will return to God.

Solomon's advice to us is, "Don't wait!" Remember God *before* these things happen—because we really don't know when death will come. Death is no respecter of persons. Rich. Poor. Black. White. Male. Female. Old. Young. Flower or weed, stalk or seed, nothing alive is out of the long reach of death's scythe.

None knew that better than H. G. Spafford.

Spafford was a successful Christian businessman who lived in Chicago in the 1800s. He had invested heavily in real estate on the shores of Lake Michigan, only to have it destroyed months later in the Chicago Fire of 1871. For weeks, Spafford and his wife helped feed, clothe, comfort, and give shelter to the homeless victims of the fire. Exhausted from the ordeal, they were counseled by a physician to take a long, relaxing trip. So Spafford planned a trip to Europe for his family and sent them on ahead while he finished up business in Chicago.

On November 22, however, during the passage over, their ship, the SS *Ville du Havre*, was struck by an English vessel and sank in twelve minutes. His wife and young daughters held on desperately to some floating pieces of wreckage, but one by one the weary daughters slipped out of their mother's grasp and into a watery grave. Several days later, the survivors finally landed in Wales, where Mrs. Spafford cabled her husband with the bittersweet news: "Saved alone." Spafford then left by ship to join his bereaved wife. At sea, he penned the words to the now popular hymn:

When peace, like a river, attendeth my way,
When sorrows like sea billows roll—
Whatever my lot, Thou hast taught me to say,
It is well, it is well with my soul.[3]

This hymn points to that peace which surpasses all understanding (see Phil. 4:7)—a peace that only Jesus can give (see John 14:27).

Solomon's Message to Us Today

Can you face death with that type of peace? Is it well with your soul? Or is your soul troubled at the thought of death, either yours or that of a loved one? Don't run away from those troubling feelings; instead, follow the counsel they and Solomon's reminders are trying to tell you: *The time to walk with God is now, not later.* As Solomon finally resolved:

The conclusion, when all has been heard, is: fear God and keep His commandments, because this applies to every person. For God will bring every act to judgment, everything which is hidden, whether it is good or evil. (Eccles. 12:13–14)

And Solomon would know.

👑 *Living Insights*   STUDY ONE

More bitter than sweet are the final entries in Solomon's diary. Ecclesiastes is a painful book, a difficult book to read . . . perhaps because the emptiness and meaninglessness Solomon writes about are things we sometimes find in ourselves when we are awake and alone in the middle of the night.

Where do these dark, despairing feelings come from? The causes are many and varied; some are simple, others very complex. They can stem from depression, loss, fear, cruel and false self-criticism, or some of the things we've seen in Solomon's life—like excess and wasted time and a defiant abandonment of God.

---

3. Horatio G. Spafford, "It Is Well with My Soul," in *101 Hymn Stories*, by Kenneth W. Osbeck (1982; reprint, Grand Rapids, Mich.: Kregel Publications, 1986), p. 126. Mr. Spafford's story is adapted from Osbeck's book and Charles L. Allen's *You Are Never Alone* (Old Tappan, N.J.: Fleming H. Revell Co., 1978), p. 94.

And one reason could be the absence of love.

Not once in Solomon's entire journal of Ecclesiastes does he look back and speak tenderly of someone he loved, someone he shared life with and cared deeply for. Not a parent, not a friend, not a mate, not a child. Not God. This man worked for himself, spent his wealth to serve himself, used many women to give pleasure to himself, forgot God and lived for himself.

His wealth and wisdom extended beyond anything the world had ever known, but *he* did not extend himself in love. And that, as the apostle Paul has written, results in emptiness.

> If I speak in the tongues of men and of angels, but have not love, I am only a resounding gong or a clanging cymbal. If I have the gift of prophecy and can fathom all mysteries and all knowledge, and if I have a faith that can move mountains, but have not love, I am nothing. If I give all I possess to the poor and surrender my body to the flames, but have not love, I gain nothing. (1 Cor. 13:1–3 NIV)

"If I . . . have not love, I am nothing. If I . . . have not love, I gain nothing." Do you think the opposite may be true, that if we do love as Christ did we could transform our empty nothingness into fullness and meaning (see John 15:9–17)?

Take time now to look at your life, as Solomon did his. Do you have any barren places of regret? Don't beat yourself up over them; the past is done. Rather, learn from them. How could love make a difference in your present and future?

If I Had It to Do All Over Again . . .

_____

_____

_____

_____

_____

_____

_____

_____

_____

_____

"Better a poor but wise youth than an old but foolish king who no longer knows how to take warning," Solomon confessed (Eccles. 4:13 NIV). Hopefully, our hearts are still young enough to be able to take the warning from this chapter of Solomon's life: *the time to walk with God is now, not later.* How is your walk with God going?

How conscious are you of your accountability to God? Does it make a difference in your motives, choices, and actions? If not, why?

_____

_____

_____

Where are your priorities? Is having right priorities a "priority" to you?

_____

_____

_____

How would you say you remember your Creator? How do you forget Him?

_____

_____

_____

How does getting older play a factor in your walk with God? Do you put off certain things until later? Do you even think about aging?

_____

_____

_____

What are your feelings about death? How does death impact your spiritual life?

_____

_____

_____

_____

_____

_____

If you are unsure of where you are with God, talk to Him about it right now. Ask Him to show you what you need to do—and for the strength to do it. If you've never accepted Christ as your Savior, can you think of a better time than now to do it? Just tell Him where you are and that you'd like Him to come into your heart and life. You don't have to "have it all together" before you come to Him. His forgiveness and power and love are there for the asking. And hope and newness of life will be yours from this day forward (see John 3:16; 2 Cor. 5:17; Eph. 2:1–10).

Chapter 7

A PLEA FOR GODLINESS
Selected Scriptures

"All of us like sheep have gone astray, Each of us has turned to his own way," the prophet Isaiah insightfully wrote (53:6). Sheep have a habit of wandering from the flock. Often a sheep moves from one clump of grass to another, so enmeshed in each green island of vegetation that no thought is given as to how far it has ventured from the fold.

Likewise, we are all, as the hymnist echoes, "prone to wander." We have seen it in Solomon; we see it in ourselves. In selfish pursuit of our own desires, we choose a way that is far from the Shepherd. And so we wander through life solitary, separated from God.

This predisposition to waywardness is a universal tendency. It is our nature—a nature that is fallen, wayward, depraved. Left to itself, this depraved nature strays from everything godly. And just like sheep, the farther we wander, the greater the dangers.

In our insatiable search for greener grass, we slip away to permissive pastures. These lead to winding trails of rationalization, which, in turn, lead to the sheer cliffs of rebellion. That's the path Solomon took when he strayed from God. But like a shepherd calling in the darkness for a lost sheep, God called to him twice; but Solomon, standing on the precipice, ignored the plea (1 Kings 11:9–10).

You may be on the precipice yourself this very moment. Or on the winding trail leading to it. Or grazing contentedly amid the seductive lushness of the permissive pasture. Wherever, God is cupping His hands and calling you, in a plea for godliness, to come home.

The Root of Depravity

At the root of depravity is a nature totally alienated from God. As a bad tree cannot produce good fruit (see Matt. 7:17–18), so the depraved roots of our nature can produce nothing that will gain God's approval.

This message was not part of the original series but is compatible with it.

For all of us have become like one who is unclean,
And all our righteous deeds are like a filthy garment.
(Isa. 64:6a)

Regardless of how moral and upstanding we view ourselves, Isaiah says we are all like the leper who has to cry out in the street "Unclean! Unclean!" so that people may get out of the way (see Lev. 13:45). And like Cain, we may proudly bring our fruit baskets of good works before the throne of God (compare Gen. 4:2–5 with Heb. 11:4), but they will lay before Him in a limp, disgusting pile, like garments stained with blood.[1]

The Fruit of Depravity

Depravity's root gives branch to a variety of thorny fruit: immorality, gossip, lying, impure thoughts, violence, thefts, and so forth. Romans 3 is a mosaic of Old Testament passages inlaid to produce a picture of our depraved nature.

As it is written,

"There is none righteous, not even one;
There is none who understands,
There is none who seeks for God;
All have turned aside, together they have become
    useless;
There is none who does good,
There is not even one."
"Their throat is an open grave,
With their tongues they keep deceiving,"
"The poison of asps is under their lips";
"Whose mouth is full of cursing and bitterness";
"Their feet are swift to shed blood,
Destruction and misery are in their paths,
And the path of peace have they not known."
"There is no fear of God before their eyes."
(vv. 10–18)

1. Isaiah's Hebrew term for "filthy garment" actually refers to "'a garment of menstruation,' *i.e.* stained by menstrual blood. Bodily discharges that were linked with procreation were considered a defilement because they were so vitally associated with fallen human life. Even what we might consider to be in our favor, *our righteous acts*, flow from a fallen nature and partake of its fallenness." J. Alec Motyer, *The Prophecy of Isaiah: An Introduction and Commentary* (Downers Grove, Ill.: InterVarsity Press, 1993), p. 520.

59

Deceit, cursing, bitterness, destruction, misery, turmoil, no fear of God. In similar fashion, Paul enumerates the deeds of the flesh in Galatians 5.

> Now the deeds of the flesh are evident, which are: immorality, impurity, sensuality, idolatry, sorcery, enmities, strife, jealousy, outbursts of anger, disputes, dissensions, factions, envying, drunkenness, carousing, and things like these, of which I forewarn you just as I have forewarned you that those who practice such things shall not inherit the kingdom of God. (vv. 19–21)

"The Scripture has shut up all men under sin," Paul writes of depravity (3:22a), but he doesn't leave us without hope:

> that the promise by faith in Jesus Christ might be given to those who believe. (v. 22b)

Only those who have put their faith in Christ have a real hope of producing anything other than depravity's fruit. For, since the nature we are born with is depraved (Rom. 5:12), the only way to produce fruit that is good in God's eyes is to receive a new nature, which we are given when we are born again. And it is this new nature that we must learn to cooperate with—which involves our will; it isn't automatic—as Paul reveals in Ephesians 4:22–24.

> In reference to your former manner of life, you lay aside the old self, which is being corrupted in accordance with the lusts of deceit, and that you be renewed in the spirit of your mind, and put on the new self, which in the likeness of God has been created in righteousness and holiness of the truth. (see also 5:8–9)

The Rationalization of Depravity

Because there is nothing pretty about our old nature, we sometimes deny the resemblance—as with the photo on our driver's license. Other times we rationalize, which *Webster's* defines as "to provide plausible but untrue reasons for conduct."[2] The mirror of Romans 3:10–18 reflects a nature that is ugly and depraved. When

2. *Merriam-Webster's Collegiate Dictionary*, 10th ed., see "rationalize."

looking into this passage, our natural tendency is to rationalize what we see—"the lighting's too bright" or "everybody looks bad in the morning."

A classic example of rationalization is shelved away in 1 Samuel 15. In this chapter, we find a soiled page in Saul's reign over Israel.

> Then Samuel said to Saul, "The Lord sent me to anoint you as king over His people, over Israel; now therefore, listen to the words of the Lord. Thus says the Lord of hosts, 'I will punish Amalek for what he did to Israel, how he set himself against him on the way while he was coming up from Egypt. Now go and strike Amalek and utterly destroy all that he has, and do not spare him; but put to death both man and woman, child and infant, ox and sheep, camel and donkey.'" (vv. 1–3)

The command was specific and clear. Saul's follow-through, however, was less than complete once the dust of battle settled.

> So Saul defeated the Amalekites, from Havilah as you go to Shur, which is east of Egypt. And he captured Agag the king of the Amalekites alive, and utterly destroyed all the people with the edge of the sword. But Saul and the people spared Agag and the best of the sheep, the oxen, the fatlings, the lambs, and all that was good, and were not willing to destroy them utterly; but everything despised and worthless, that they utterly destroyed. (vv. 7–9)

God responded to Saul's disobedience with deep regret.

> Then the word of the Lord came to Samuel, saying, "I regret that I have made Saul king, for he has turned back from following Me, and has not carried out My commands." And Samuel was distressed and cried out to the Lord all night. (vv. 10–11)

When the weary prophet went to confront Saul the next morning, he was met with an amazingly oblivious greeting.

> And Samuel came to Saul, and Saul said to him, "Blessed are you of the Lord! I have carried out the command of the Lord." (v. 13)

How could the king say such a thing? That's just what Samuel wondered too, and he wasn't about to let Saul get away with such a lie.

> But Samuel said, "What then is this bleating of the
> sheep in my ears, and the lowing of the oxen which
> I hear?" (v. 14)

Now squirming in his sandals, Saul hastily created a flimsy rationalization.

> And Saul said, "They have brought them from the
> Amalekites, for the people spared the best of the
> sheep and oxen, to sacrifice to the Lord your God;
> but the rest we have utterly destroyed." (v. 15)

"The people did it, Samuel, not me," said Saul as he vainly tried to blame his way out of the problem. Samuel's response, however, pointed the accusing finger back where it belonged and drove to the root of Saul's rebellious nature.

> "Why then did you not obey the voice of the Lord,
> but rushed upon the spoil and did what was evil in
> the sight of the Lord? . . .
> Has the Lord as much delight in burnt
>   offerings and sacrifices
> As in obeying the voice of the Lord?
> Behold, to obey is better than sacrifice,
> And to heed than the fat of rams.
> For rebellion is as the sin of divination,
> And insubordination is as iniquity and
>   idolatry.
> Because you have rejected the word of the
>   Lord,
> He has also rejected you from being king."
> (vv. 19, 22–23)

Clearly, with God our depravity and rebellion are no light matters to be rationalized away. His words are strong, and they are irrevocable. But sure as His judgments are, His guidance into the way of life is even surer.

Opposing Our Depravity

As we have seen in Solomon's and Saul's lives—as well as in our own—depravity has a gravitational pull that leads downward to rebellion. If the righteous nature is ignored, permissiveness results. Permissiveness then leads to rationalization when holiness is ignored. And rationalization leads to rebellion when repentance is ignored.

How, then, can we combat the descending gravity of our depraved nature? The apostle Peter gives us some powerful counsel in his first letter.

> Therefore, gird your minds for action, keep sober in spirit, fix your hope completely on the grace to be brought to you at the revelation of Jesus Christ. As obedient children, do not be conformed to the former lusts which were yours in your ignorance.
> (1 Pet. 1:13–14)

Notice where all the action starts: "your minds." And notice how active the verbs are: "*gird* your minds . . . *keep* sober in spirit . . . *fix* your hope" (emphasis added). If we are to live in godliness, above the destruction of depravity, it will require a conscious mental effort. It will require obedience to God and at the same time resistance to being conformed to the depravity within us.

The "former lusts" in verse 14 are the fruit of our old nature, which, like a magnet, would continually draw us back there to feed. This tug-of-war between the flesh and the Spirit is hostile and constant (see Gal. 5:17). The rope is always taut. Simply becoming a Christian and receiving a new nature does not guarantee victory—at least, not without a struggle. But it is not impossible, or Peter wouldn't have given us this next objective:

> But like the Holy One who called you, be holy yourselves also in all your behavior; because it is written, "You shall be holy, for I am holy."
> (1 Pet. 1:15–16)

These verses are both a call to arms and a plea for godliness—a plea to be like and to reverence the Holy One who has called us.

Strategy for Godliness

Since godliness is achievable but doesn't come naturally, we need to have an effective strategy in place. The following three action points can help us begin to supplant depravity's sway over us.

First, *when depravity tends to lead you down the permissive path, take God seriously.* Peter again gives us clear instructions:

> And if you address as Father the One who impartially judges according to each man's work, conduct yourselves in fear during the time of your stay upon earth. (v. 17)

The key idea is healthy *fear.* Paul echoes his fellow apostle's thought, saying that we will reap what we have sown because "God is not mocked" (Gal. 6:7). He is holy. He is just. And He is to be taken seriously.

Second, *when permissiveness tends to make you rationalize, then pursue God vigorously.* Like Saul, when we've done wrong and are faced directly with it, lies and blame seem to spring out of nowhere as we desperately try to get out of that uncomfortable spot. Our key idea, then, needs to be *honesty.* We need to follow hard after God's desire for our purity and maturity, and that means telling the truth—come what may (see Ps. 51:6).

And third, *instead of rebelling, submit to God willingly.* God's grace covers many things, but we are not to take it for granted. We cannot presume that God will overlook deliberate, continued sin—like adultery, abuse, or deceit, for example. Both Saul and Solomon had their kingdoms taken from them because of their rebellion, remember? Samuel's pained words to Saul need to pierce our hearts as well.

> "Has the Lord as much delight in burnt offerings
>   and sacrifices
> As in obeying the voice of the Lord?"
> (1 Sam. 15:22a)

The key idea here is *humility.* Rebellion is a prideful resisting of God's rightful authority. And as James says, "God is opposed to the proud, but gives grace to the humble" (James 4:6). Only a heart that is humble before our holy, loving God is open to His grace . . . which He longs to give to us, if we are only willing (see Isa. 30:18).

Living Insights

Depravity versus godliness—which seems to be winning in your life? The thorns and thistles of depravity's fruit aren't always jumping out at us in neon lights, saying, "Thorn here! Thistle straight ahead!" No, they're usually much more subtle, like the slender, green needles concealed under the lush foliage of a beautiful bougainvillea. They can be little white thorns of lying, plausible thorns of rationalizing, subtle thorns of permissiveness. Recognize any?

Are you starting to go astray in a permissive pasture? In what areas of your life have you noticed this?

Are you taking God's call to holiness seriously, or are you presuming on His grace? Do you even think of Him at all when that lenient way beckons? How is the reality of God figuring in your thoughts?

Are you good at rationalizing? When you are cornered about what you've permitted in your life, do you evade personal responsibility by bending the truth to keep yourself safe? Do you try to hide behind the excuse that it's somebody else's fault?

Where is your heart for the Lord while this is going on?

A thorn less easy to hide is rebellion, but the world helps us out here. Being a rebel is quite fashionable; it sells jeans, garners more volume on the sitcom laugh track, creates such beauties as MTV. It looks independent, decisive, strong. It takes the initiative, but it doesn't take any guff from anybody. It has attitude and style. Does it have you? What do you notice?

_____

_____

_____

Does your life reveal any areas that proudly oppose God? Does humility before Him seem as appealing to you as playing the rebel?

_____

_____

_____

Depravity is pretty sneaky, isn't it? But it's not invincible. The thorns can be rooted out with God's power, and He'll, in turn, give us new soil for our souls from which everlasting fruit can grow.

👑 Living Insights

STUDY TWO

Our overall study of Solomon's life has put us knee-deep in depravity, hasn't it? We've seen it in his disobedience, idolatry, extravagance, and rebellion; and in this chapter we've examined depravity's roots and its fruit. And it is right that we have studied this in such detail, for if we're going to fight against something, we must first know exactly what it looks like.

By the same token, though, we also need to be just as attuned to what we are fighting for. So let's step out of the thorns and thistles, muck and mire of depravity and spend some time acquainting ourselves with the garden of godliness.

According to Galatians 5:22–23, what kind of fruit can you expect to find in this garden?

_____

_____

_____

What blossoms does Ephesians 4:15, 32 reveal?

_____

_____

And Colossians 2:12–15—what blooms do you find there?

_____

_____

_____

_____

_____

Have you ever seen such a beautiful seed catalogue in your life? And have you ever realized that it is God who brings each of these tender, precious plants into existence? That because of Him we have these qualities, which we cherish, in our world at all?

Being like Him, being godly—Godlike—is a worthy life's goal, isn't it? "Be holy, for I am holy." The apostle Paul put this in similar words, which are, perhaps, more approachable:

> Therefore be imitators of God, as beloved children; and walk in love, just as Christ also loved you, and gave Himself up for us, an offering and a sacrifice to God as a fragrant aroma. (Eph. 5:1–2)

How does your garden grow? God is in the business of transplanting and transforming. Consult Him about the landscaping of your life today, won't you? You won't be disappointed!

Chapter 8

NEEDED:
A GODLY MIND

Ephesians 6:10–13; 2 Corinthians 2:10–11; 4:3–4; 10:3–5

The mind is the Gettysburg of a very uncivil war between God and Satan. It is the war-torn battlefield of choice where good and evil square off. It is here that conscience unsheathes its sword to clash against expedience, that conviction bares its arm against temptation, that character raises its flag against corruption. Every important battle is first fought in the mind.

Theft occurs in thought before it ever lays hands on its coveted object. Adultery is consummated in the brain before it ever enters the bedroom. Murder lurks in the dark alleys of the mind before it actually kills its victim. Ultimately, all of life's battles are either won or lost in the mind.

Because the stakes are so high, the competition to gain control of this territory is keen. Describing the battle of his conversion from atheism to Christianity, C. S. Lewis recollects:

> A young man who wishes to remain a sound Atheist cannot be too careful of his reading. There are traps everywhere—"Bibles laid open, millions of surprises," as Herbert says, "fine nets and stratagems." God is, if I may say it, very unscrupulous.[1]

But Satan, too, is cunning in his methods, as Paul says in 2 Corinthians 2:11, "in order that no advantage be taken of us by Satan; for we are not ignorant of his schemes." Nets . . . stratagems . . . schemes. The battle is real. God and Satan are vying for the most strategic territory in all the world—your mind.

Elements of the Battle

In Ephesians 6, Paul takes us into the council chamber of

This message was not part of the original series but is compatible with it.

1. C. S. Lewis, *Surprised by Joy* (New York, N.Y.: Harcourt Brace Jovanovich, 1955), p. 191.

heaven, where the war is mapped, enemy movements are charted, and strategies are discussed.

The Battle Cry

Paul rallies the Christian warrior with these stirring words:

> Finally, be strong in the Lord, and in the strength of His might. (v. 10)

Notice where our strength lies—not in ourselves but "in the Lord, and in . . . His might."

The Battle Strategy

Continuing, Paul instructs us on how to employ God's strength.

> Put on the full armor of God, that you may be able to stand firm against the schemes of the devil. . . . Therefore, take up the full armor of God, that you may be able to resist in the evil day, and having done everything, to stand firm. (vv. 11, 13)

Note again that it is not *our* armor but the armor *of God* we are to put on. The battle is spiritual; therefore, for the weapons to be effective, they, too, must be spiritual. If, for example, the enemy were an invading bacteria, the defense would be white blood cells or penicillin. If the enemy were an invading army, the defense would include guns, tanks, and planes. But when the enemy is the devil, the only defense is the armor of God.

Notice, too, what God's armor enables us to do: "stand firm" (see also v. 14). Standing firm is the only victorious posture Christians can assume when confronted by Satan and his emissaries. We must resist the devil with firm resolve, though our instincts beg us to retreat. It is true that our "adversary, the devil, prowls about like a roaring lion, seeking someone to devour" (1 Pet. 5:8). But when we resist him with the armor of God, *he* is the one who will flee (James 4:7), and we will stand secure in the power of God.

The Battleground

Paul now begins unrolling the map of spiritual warfare to reveal the enemy's hiding places.

> For our struggle is not against flesh and blood, but

against the rulers, against the powers, against the world forces of this darkness, against the spiritual forces of wickedness in the heavenly places. (v. 12)

Our enemy is not the people who oppose us but an organized hierarchy of demonic rulers, powers, and forces of darkness and wickedness whose activities originate in the heavenly places. And what is their target? *We are.* Our minds are in the cross hairs of Satan's scope. His mission: assassination.

Focus of the Battle

In order to repel our adversary, we must first know which direction he's coming from. We must spot him before he pounces on us.

Satan's Schemes

Second Corinthians 2:10–11, which expresses Paul's warning to forgive and welcome back a repentant sinner, uncovers one of Satan's hiding places and further reveals his strategy against us.

> But whom you forgive anything, I forgive also; for indeed what I have forgiven, if I have forgiven anything, I did it for your sakes in the presence of Christ, in order that no *advantage* be taken of us by Satan; for we are not ignorant of his *schemes.* (emphasis added)

The word *advantage* is from the Greek *pleonekteō*, meaning "to take advantage of, to gain, to overreach."[2] When we fail to forgive or harbor anger, for instance, we give Satan an advantage . . . an open door . . . an entrance (see also Eph. 4:26–27). We lay out a welcome mat for him to get the better of us by his crafty methods or *schemes.*

Perhaps Paul was not ignorant of Satan's schemes, but too many of us today are. This word—in Greek, *noēma*, which means "thought, purpose"—has at its root the term *nous*, meaning "mind."[3] In other words, Paul does not want us to be "ignorant of

2. Archibald Thomas Robertson, *Word Pictures in the New Testament* (Grand Rapids, Mich.: Baker Book House, 1931), vol. 4, p. 217.

3. Gerhard Kittel and Gerhard Friedrich, eds., *Theological Dictionary of the New Testament,* translated and abridged by Geoffrey W. Bromiley (1985; reprint, Grand Rapids, Mich.: William B. Eerdmans Publishing Co., 1992), p. 637.

the fact that Satan has his sights set on our minds."[4] Satan will take advantage of us by using whatever he has at hand, be it unresolved personal conflicts or consuming bitterness, to draw our minds away from God.

As C. S. Lewis rightly observed, the mind will be occupied either with the things of God or with things that delight the devil:

> There is no neutral ground in the universe: every square inch, every split second, is claimed by God and counterclaimed by Satan.[5]

Whose flag is planted in your mind? If your mind is filled with anger and bitterness, the colors flying indicate that the territory is occupied by the enemy. Burn that flag, won't you? Bury the bitterness. Let love do its spadework to cover the multitude of sins committed against you by that offending person. And raise a new flag, Christ's banner, over that war-ravaged territory!

Satan's Method

Two chapters down, in 2 Corinthians 4, Paul uncovers the condition of our minds before we joined forces with Christ.

> And even if our gospel is veiled, it is veiled to those who are perishing, in whose case the god of this world has blinded the minds of the unbelieving, that they might not see the light of the gospel of the glory of Christ, who is the image of God. (vv. 3–4)

Before we were saved, all of our perceptions, attitudes, patterns of thought were formed in blindness. God's deliverance and way of life were veiled, kept from us by Satan. When Christ came into our lives, though, He penetrated the part of our mind that can grasp the need for repentance and the hope He offers.

However, other parts of our minds are still veiled. We don't become automatically mature the moment we accept Christ; learning to walk in His ways and grow in His holiness takes time. And it takes persistence to uncover and lay before Him our entrenched, blind ways of thinking and relating.

4. From the study guide *Living Above the Level of Mediocrity*, rev. ed., originally coauthored by Ken Gire, from the Bible-teaching ministry of Charles R. Swindoll (Anaheim, Calif.: Insight for Living, 1994), p. 3.

5. C. S. Lewis, *Christian Reflections* (Grand Rapids, Mich.: William B. Eerdmans Publishing Co., 1967), p. 33.

For example, if, over the course of my life, I have cultivated the habits of lust and permissiveness and sensuality, I am still prone to be a lustful and sensual individual. If anger has been my way of life, then I still have a wall of anger for Christ to overcome. The Holy Spirit longs to break down that wall, peel back that veil, and take control; but it isn't automatic. We don't simply forget past patterns; they must be captured and vanquished by Christ.

Satan Besieged

In order for Christ to conquer the territory of a blinded and imprisoned mind, He must penetrate the walls built by Satan. And to do so, He must use the right weaponry.

> For though we walk in the flesh, we do not war according to the flesh, for the weapons of our warfare are not of the flesh, but divinely powerful for the destruction of fortresses. (2 Cor. 10:3–4)

Rifles, revolvers, knives, and bombs are futile, fleshly weapons against the lifestyle of the world. We aren't waging war against the flesh, remember, but against "the *spiritual* forces of wickedness" (Eph. 6:12). Against spiritual, unseen enemies we need spiritual weapons. And one of the most "divinely powerful" is the Word of God.

This is one of our few offensive weapons, which is listed at the end of Paul's itemized arsenal in Ephesians 6—"The sword of the Spirit, which is the word of God" (v. 17).

Like the sword Excalibur in the Arthurian legends, the Word of God carries with it a certain enchantment. It cuts and penetrates like no earthly weapon:

> For the word of God is living and active and sharper than any two-edged sword, and piercing as far as the division of soul and spirit, of both joints and marrow, and able to judge the thoughts and intentions of the heart. (Heb. 4:12)

We can no more succeed in battle without this weapon arming our minds and memories than a sailor can go into battle without a ship. In both cases, we'd be sunk.

What, precisely, are the targets of our weapons? They are described, metaphorically, as "fortresses." This word picture is drawn from ancient biblical history, when strategic cities were surrounded by fortified walls of defense. Within these walls were carefully placed towers, built higher than the highest point of the surrounding wall. They served as observation posts for the battle strategists, who were flanked by buglers who sent signals to the soldiers. For a city to be conquered, the walls had to be scaled, the towers seized, and the strategists captured.

Our minds are the fortresses, and in the next verse Paul shows us what has to happen inside them to claim Satan's territory for Christ.

> [The weapons of our warfare are] destroying specu-
> lations and every lofty thing raised up against the
> knowledge of God, and we are taking every thought
> captive to the obedience of Christ.[6] (2 Cor. 10:5)

The Greek word for *speculations* is derived from the same root from which we get our word *logic*. The logic of the world's system finds reasonable-sounding ways to make wrong appear right. Adultery becomes finding one's true love; pride becomes strong-minded independence; intolerance becomes political correctness.

God's Word gives no place to human speculation. He has no doubt about what is right and what is wrong, about what is true and what is false, about what is life and what is death. So He determinedly uses His living and powerful Word to destroy the speculations that would imprison us, as well as tear down "every lofty thing" that would ensnare us.

The "lofty things" work hand in hand with the speculations, only their job is to take away the guilt of wrongdoing. They are the things that say, "That's OK, everybody does that. . . . It's not your fault, your parents were creeps. . . . Compared to those guys, you're an angel!" Excusing, blaming, and comparing all work very hard to free us from the truth. But in reality, the most freeing thing we can do is bring our thoughts captive to the Truth, Jesus Christ (see John 14:6).

Encouragement for the Battle

The weapons God uses to penetrate our mental walls are in total contradiction to the world's logic.

> For the word of the cross is to those who are

---

6. The words "We are" at the beginning of the verse do not appear in the original Greek text but have been supplied by later editors. It is in the strength of God's weapons, not our own, that we can gain victory in the mind.

perishing foolishness, but to us who are being saved it is the power of God. For it is written,
"I will destroy the wisdom of the wise,
And the cleverness of the clever I will set aside."
Where is the wise man? Where is the scribe? Where is the debater of this age? Has not God made foolish the wisdom of the world? For since in the wisdom of God the world through its wisdom did not come to know God, God was well-pleased through the foolishness of the message preached to save those who believe. (1 Cor. 1:18–21)

The logic of God is sacrificial love; His battering ram, a blood-stained cross.

With the battering ram of the Cross and the sword of the Spirit (Eph. 6:17; Heb. 4:12), Satan's fortresses can be destroyed; the enemy, evicted. Thoughts, once enslaved, can be emancipated to serve the Lord Jesus—"and you shall know the truth, and the truth shall make you free" (John 8:32).

👑 Living Insights STUDY ONE

Are you fired up for battle now? Before you charge into enemy territory, let's make sure you're fully equipped and all your weapons are in place. In this study, we'll look at the first four armaments listed in Ephesians 6:14–16; then, in our next study, we'll finish up the last three in verses 17–18. Ready? Then stand for inspection!

• "Stand firm, therefore, having girded your loins with truth." Truth is our first weapon. Are there areas in your life—ways of thinking, fears, hurt feelings—that a true and right perspective could liberate? What are they? Bring those lies out into the light by writing them down.

_____

_____

Are there any false ideas trying to separate you from God's love and presence? Name them; and if any Scriptures come to mind that counter them, write down their references.

- "And having put on the breastplate of righteousness." Guarding the heart is righteousness. How just and fair are your decisions, whether in your business dealings or in your relationships? How merciful and compassionate are they?

Is your righteousness formed by and modeled after Christ's? Is it humble or self-righteous?

- "And having shod your feet with the preparation of the gospel of peace." Our footing is firm because our walk is established in Christ's peace. What tends to rattle your peace with Christ? Feelings of unworthiness? Doubts? Hurts, whether past or present, that you don't understand?

Do you try your best to build peace with others? Or are strife and unresolved conflict dominating factors in your life? How well are you living out your reconciling peace with God?

- "In addition to all, taking up the shield of faith with which you will be able to extinguish all the flaming missiles of the evil one." Holding fast to our belief in God's promises and character protects us from having our lives burned up. When trouble after trouble, arrow after arrow, comes your way, how sturdy a shield is your faith? Is God still a good God when you are frightened or in pain?

_____

_____

Don't we all want relief from the battle more than standing and fighting it out? What has happened to you when your weary arms have dropped the shield of faith? Are those moments you are proud of or do they hold a burning regret? What did they do to your testimony, your confidence before God?

_____

_____

Living Insights

Let's continue our inspection now by focusing on the weapons laid out for us in Ephesians 6:17–18.

- "And take the helmet of salvation." Our minds are especially protected by the hope of salvation. Are you more prone to hope or despair? Is life more impossible than possible to you?

_____

_____

Does God's saving power figure often in your thinking? How real and sure and joyful is your salvation to you?

_____

_____

- "And the sword of the Spirit, which is the word of God." God's words given to us in Scripture are wielded on our behalf by the very Spirit of God. How firm a grasp do you have on God's words? Is this sword a ready weapon for the hands of the Spirit or are the edges blunted and dull?

_____

76

Is God's message to you made of living words? Or do you look at the Bible as an antique yet holy thing? What is your attitude, and how does it affect your motivation to be well armed?

_____

_____

- "With all prayer and petition pray at all times in the Spirit, and with this in view, be on the alert with all perseverance and petition for all the saints." Prayer is integral to the success of all these weapons; yet how often do we read God's Word or try to do right or muster up positive, hopeful thinking without linking our hearts first to His? How would you describe your prayer life? Is it honest? Is it a priority?

_____

_____

How persevering are your prayers? What relationship have you seen in your life between praying and your ability to stand firm?

_____

_____

Now that you know the state of your armor, both the strengths and the chinks, you are that much readier for battle. This last weapon of prayer is what can help you shore up those weaker areas and make the most of the strong ones. So use it, won't you? Ask God for His guidance and help in making you a fully equipped soldier of the Cross.

BOOKS FOR
PROBING FURTHER

S olomon was a restless man, going from woman to woman, project to project, pleasure to pleasure. Is your heart, like Solomon's, restless? In his *Confessions*, Augustine bares his heart before God: "You have made us for yourself, and our hearts are restless till they find their rest in you."[1] Maybe you're seeking rest in the wrong pastures. Maybe you're spending too much time looking for greener grass and not enough time looking for your Shepherd. Is your heart, like Solomon's, unfulfilled? Maybe you're filling it with the wrong things—experiences that titillate the tastebuds but don't stick to your spiritual ribs. Essentially, Solomon's problem wasn't wine, women, and song. Or wealth. Or power. It was a problem of the heart.

I hope our studies on Solomon have convinced you of the importance of maintaining a close relationship with God. Nothing else can take His place in your heart. Nothing. And I hope you have the opportunity to read the books listed below. I think they will go a long way in helping you develop a heart that beats for God.

Briscoe, Stuart D. *Playing by the Rules*. Old Tappan, N.J.: Fleming H. Revell Co., 1986.

Lewis, C. S. *The Screwtape Letters*. New York, N.Y.: Macmillan Publishing Co., 1961.

Swindoll, Charles R. *Living on the Ragged Edge*. Waco, Tex.: Word Books, Publisher, 1985.

White, John. *The Golden Cow*. Downers Grove, Ill.: InterVarsity Press, 1979.

Some of these books may be out of print and available only through a library. For those currently available, please contact your local Christian bookstore. Books by Charles R. Swindoll may be obtained through Insight for Living. IFL also offers some books by other authors—please note the ordering information that follows and contact the office that serves you.

1. St. Augustine, *The Confessions of Augustine in Modern English*, trans. and ed. Sherwood E. Wirt (1971; reprint, Grand Rapids, Mich.: Zondervan Publishing House, Clarion Classics, 1986), p. 1.

ORDERING INFORMATION

SOLOMON

Cassette Tapes and Study Guide

This Bible study guide was designed to be used independently or in conjunction with the broadcast of Chuck Swindoll's taped messages which are listed below. If you would like to order cassette tapes or further copies of this study guide, please see the information given below and the order form provided at the end of this guide.

		U.S.	Canada
SOL	Study guide	$ 3.95 ea.	$ 5.25 ea.
SOLCS	Cassette series, includes all individual tapes, album cover, and one complimentary study guide	29.20	36.75 ea.
SOL 1-4	Individual cassettes, includes messages A and B	6.30 ea.	8.00 ea.

The prices are subject to change without notice.

SOL 1-A: *Stepping into Big Sandals*—Selected Scriptures
       B: *Solomon in Living Color*—Selected Scriptures from 1 Kings

SOL 2-A: *Signs of Erosion*—Selected Scriptures
       B: *When the Heart Is Turned Away*—1 Kings 11:1–9

SOL 3-A: *How God Deals with Defiance*—1 Kings 11:9–28, 40
       B: *Sound Advice from an Old Rebel*—Ecclesiastes 11:9–12:7

SOL 4-A: *A Plea for Godliness**—Selected Scriptures
       B: *Needed: A Godly Mind**—Ephesians 6:10–13; 2 Corinthians 2:10–11; 4:3–4; 10:3–5

*These messages were not part of the original series but are compatible with it.

How to Order by Phone or FAX

(Credit card orders only)

United States: 1-800-772-8888 from 7:00 A.M. to 4:30 P.M., Pacific time, Monday through Friday
FAX (714) 575-5496 anytime, day or night

Canada: 1-800-663-7639, Vancouver residents call (604) 596-2910 from 7:00 A.M. to 5:00 P.M., Pacific time, Monday through Friday FAX (604) 596-2975 anytime, day or night

Australia: (03) 872-4606 or FAX (03) 874-8890 from 8:00 A.M. to 5:00 P.M., Monday through Friday

Other International Locations: call the Ordering Services Department in the United States at (714) 575-5000 during the hours listed above.

How to Order by Mail

United States
- Mail to: Ordering Services Department
  Insight for Living
  Post Office Box 69000
  Anaheim, CA 92817-0900
- Sales tax: California residents add 7.25%.
- Shipping: add 10% of the total order amount for first-class delivery. (Otherwise, allow four to six weeks for fourth-class delivery.)
- Payment: personal checks, money orders, credit cards (Visa, Master-Card, Discover Card, and American Express). No invoices or COD orders available.
- $10 fee for *any* returned check.

Canada
- Mail to: Insight for Living Ministries
  Post Office Box 2510
  Vancouver, BC V6B 3W7
- Sales tax: please add 7% GST. British Columbia residents also add 7% sales tax (on tapes or cassette series).
- Shipping: included in prices listed above.
- Payment: personal checks, money orders, credit cards (Visa, Master-Card). No invoices or COD orders available.
- Delivery: approximately four weeks.

Australia and the South Pacific
- Mail to: Insight for Living, Inc.
  GPO Box 2823 EE
  Melbourne, Victoria 3001, Australia
- Shipping: add 25% to the total order.
- Delivery: approximately four to six weeks.

- Payment: personal checks payable in Australian funds, international money orders, or credit cards (Visa, MasterCard, and BankCard).

Other International Locations
- Mail to: Ordering Services, International
  Insight for Living
  Post Office Box 69000
  Anaheim, CA 92817-0900
- Shipping and delivery time: please see chart that follows.
- Payment: personal checks payable in U.S. funds, international money orders, or credit cards (Visa, MasterCard, and American Express).

Type of Shipping	Postage Cost	Delivery
Surface	10% of total order*	6 to 10 weeks
Airmail	25% of total order*	under 6 weeks

*Use U.S. price as a base.

Our Guarantee

Your complete satisfaction is our top priority here at Insight for Living. If you're not completely satisfied with anything you order, please return it for full credit, a refund, or a replacement, as you prefer.

Insight for Living Catalog

The Insight for Living catalog features study guides, tapes, and books by a variety of Christian authors. To obtain a free copy, call us at the numbers listed above.

Order Form
United States, Australia, and Other International Locations
(Canadian residents please use order form on reverse side.)

SOLCS represents the entire *Solomon* series in a special album cover, while SOL 1–4 are the individual tapes included in the series. SOL represents this study guide, should you desire to order additional copies.

SOL	Study guide	$ 3.95 ea.
SOLCS	Cassette series,	29.20
	includes all individual tapes, album cover, and one complimentary study guide	
SOL 1–4	Individual cassettes, includes messages A and B	6.30 ea.

Product Code	Product Description	Quantity	Unit Price	Total
			$	$
	Subtotal			
	California Residents—Sales Tax *Add 7.25% of subtotal.*			
	U.S. First-Class Shipping *For faster delivery, add 10% for postage and handling.*			
	Non-United States Residents *Australia add 25% for shipping and handling.* *All other locations: U.S. price plus 10% surface postage or 25% airmail.*			
	Gift to Insight for Living *Tax-deductible in the United States.*			
	Total Amount Due *Please do not send cash.*		$	

Prices are subject to change without notice.

Payment by: ❑ Check or money order payable to Insight for Living ❑ Credit card

(Circle one):   Visa   MasterCard   Discover Card   American Express

Number _____

Expiration Date _____ Signature _____
We cannot process your credit card purchase without your signature.

Name _____

Address _____

City _____ State _____

Zip Code _____ Country _____

Telephone (____) _____ Radio Station ____ ____ ____ ____
If questions arise concerning your order, we may need to contact you.

Mail this order form to the Ordering Services Department at one of these addresses:

Insight for Living
Post Office Box 69000, Anaheim, CA 92817-0900

Insight for Living, Inc.
GPO Box 2823 EE, Melbourne, VIC 3001, Australia

Order Form
Canadian Residents
(Residents of the United States, Australia, and other international locations, please use order form on reverse side.)

SOLCS represents the entire *Solomon* series in a special album cover, while SOL 1–4 are the individual tapes included in the series. SOL represents this study guide, should you desire to order additional copies.

SOL	Study guide	$ 5.25 ea.
SOLCS	Cassette series, includes all individual tapes, album cover, and one complimentary study guide	36.75
SOL 1–4	Individual cassettes, includes messages A and B	8.00 ea.

Product Code	Product Description	Quantity	Unit Price	Total
			$	$
		Subtotal		
		Add 7% GST		
		British Columbia Residents Add 7% sales tax on individual tapes or cassette series.		
		Gift to Insight for Living Ministries Tax-deductible in Canada.		
		Total Amount Due Please do not send cash.	$	

Prices are subject to change without notice.

Payment by: ❑ Check or money order payable to Insight for Living Ministries
❑ Credit card

(Circle one): Visa   MasterCard   Number_____

Expiration Date_____   Signature_____
We cannot process your credit card purchase without your signature.

Name_____

Address_____

City_____ Province_____

Postal Code_____ Country_____

Telephone (____)_____ Radio Station____ ____ ____ ____
If questions arise concerning your order, we may need to contact you.

Mail this order form to the Ordering Services Department at the following address:

Insight for Living Ministries
Post Office Box 2510
Vancouver, BC, Canada V6B 3W7